D1168772

GOD'S PLAN
FOR OUR
GOOD

Foundations
OF THE Faith

Romans
8:28

GOD'S PLAN
FOR OUR
GOOD

Paul Smith

MOODY PRESS
CHICAGO

ISBN: 0-8024-3077-5

3 5 7 9 10 8 6 4 2

Printed in the United States of America

This book is dedicated to the individuals
in the congregations I have served
in Seattle, Washington, and McKeesport, Pennsylvania,
who have inspired me with their courage and faith
as they have walked through the darkest of valleys,
putting into action the truths
we are learning together from God's Word

CONTENTS

ACKNOWLEDGMENTS

...out becoming indebted
...n possibly be acknowl-
...My wife, Carreen, likely
...ost sacrifices during the
...Our congregation at West
...Seattle pray for me and
...n. My secretary, Lynda
...rs transcribing, correct-
...pt. James S. Bell Jr. from
...to pursue this in-depth
...eryl Dunlop, my editor,
...aying effectively what I

ACKNOWLEDGMENTS

No one writes a book without becoming indebted to more people than can possibly be acknowledged. Let me mention a few. My wife, Carreen, likely has been asked to make the most sacrifices during the preparation of this manuscript. Our congregation at West Side Presbyterian Church in Seattle pray for me and allow me to practice on them. My secretary, Lynda Hurst, has put in countless hours transcribing, correcting, and preparing the manuscript. James S. Bell Jr. from Moody Press encouraged me to pursue this in-depth study of Romans 8:28. And Cheryl Dunlop, my editor, has helped me immensely in saying effectively what I mean to say.

Section One

THE PROBLEM

Chapter One

HOW COULD GOD LET THIS HAPPEN?

Psalm 22:1–11

There are moments in our lives when the huge, pitiless oppressiveness of our universe rolls over us with inescapable force. One of those moments struck me recently as I stood praying in the children's intensive care unit of a local hospital. In my left hand I held the hand of a vibrant and beautiful eleven-year-old girl. In my right I held the warm but unresponsive hand of her nine-year-old sister, equally beautiful, but slowly slipping toward what seemed to us a tragic and untimely death—the result of a sudden and traumatic brain hemorrhage. A few days earlier she had been dancing through the house, excitedly demonstrating her latest ballet techniques. Now she lay pale and still, unable to resist the menacing approach of the angel of death. The question on the heart of every person in that room was, "How could God let this happen?"

It wasn't the first time that question had been asked, nor would it be the last. In John 11:32, another young woman, Mary, had just watched her brother die. "Lord," she said to Jesus when He arrived, "if you had been here, my brother would not have died." The question was implicit, but it was the same as ours: How could You let this happen? You might have done something about it. Jesus was clearly moved by the pain this question represented. The Scripture says, "He was deeply moved in spirit and troubled" (v. 33). It hurt to see people grieving and bewildered.

We ask the question when malevolent teens murder their classmates, when ethnic groups are viciously massacred, when vulnerable women and children are assaulted. *God, how could You let this happen?* We ask it when hurricanes or tidal waves or fires or other natural disasters destroy lives and property and, perhaps worst of all, hope. *God, how could You let that happen?* We ask it when we lose our jobs or find our reputations damaged by false accusations, or even when we make foolish choices. *God, how could You let this happen?* Couldn't You have intervened? Couldn't You have saved us this pain?

I will not presume to judge anyone who asks the question. It is easy enough to challenge the questioner when all is well in our own lives. Perhaps we will be strong enough to resist the question even when things are not going so well. But when someone who appears innocent suffers the consequences of a tragedy that God alone might have prevented, it is almost impossible to avoid the question, God, how could You let this happen? The question haunts us most deeply when it involves someone we know and love. "If *I* could have prevented it, *I* would have done everything in my power, at whatever cost. Why wouldn't God have done the same?"

OUR TRUE ASSUMPTIONS ABOUT GOD'S GOODNESS

Two fundamental, true assumptions lie behind this question. (1) God is supposed to be *good;* and (2) God is supposed to be *sovereign,* or all-powerful. But here a "bad" thing has obviously happened. When bad things happen to good people, obviously (we reason) God must have failed either to be *good* or to exercise His *sovereignty.*

At first glance, it seems difficult to argue with this conclusion, and we find ourselves becoming angry with God for allowing something even *we* would not have allowed. But there is a problem with standing in judgment of God. He Himself is the standard by which all things are judged. We do not know good apart from God. His actions are the very definition of good. To complain that God has done something that He ought not to have done is rather like complaining that the sun came up too late to start the day. The day is defined by the rising of the sun, even as good is defined by the actions of God. Where could we find another standard by which to judge the actions of God? To presume that *we* can judge God is to place ourselves over God.

But even if we could justify our accusation, I don't think we want to go there. If God is *not* good—if by some higher standard He may be accused of evil—then our situation is utterly and finally hopeless. What imaginable hope could there be if the sovereign force behind the universe were monstrously evil? And if He is not sovereign —if the God responsible for running the universe can't handle it—then once again the implications are absolutely staggering. Those who draw this conclusion, or who conclude that God must not exist at all, cannot but end in

15

utter despair, for the universe is then careening out of control and we shall all inevitably become its hapless victims.

Two other possible explanations for why God allows pain and suffering have consistently been advanced, but in the end they too prove insupportable. One is that if a person suffers, God must be punishing that person for something bad he has done. Although it is true that God, like any loving parent or just judge, punishes evil, this will simply not do as an explanation for all suffering. The earliest statement of this explanation is in the Old Testament where Job had lost his crops, his flocks and herds, his children, and finally his own health. Job's friends insisted that he must have done something terrible to bring such suffering on himself. But in the end, without giving any alternate explanation, God revealed in no uncertain terms that Job had been a righteous man and that his friends were absolutely wrong in accusing him.

Jesus challenged His own disciples when they advanced the same theory in Luke 13. After certain men from Galilee had been brutally massacred, Jesus said, "Do you think that these Galileans were worse sinners than all the other Galileans because they suffered this way? I tell you, no! But unless you repent, you too will all perish. Or those eighteen who died when the tower in Siloam fell on them," Jesus volunteered (vv. 2–4a), referring to some disaster in the news, "do you think they were more guilty than all the others living in Jerusalem? I tell you, no!" (vv. 4b–5a). You see, that's not the only explanation for suffering, God says.

And if these examples are not enough, there is the image of Jesus Himself, in enormous pain, impaled on a Roman cross, and quoting Psalm 22:1, "My God, my

God, why have you forsaken me?" Jesus is surely innocent!

"Ah, but," you say, "He *was* suffering the punishment for sin on the cross." True, but not His own sin. Sin and suffering are certainly loose in the world. But what we see at the cross is an innocent victim, and as well a refusal on God's part to intervene and spare His innocent Son from the suffering inherent in a broken world. It is simply impossible, in the light of Scripture, to say that when a person suffers pain or grief or loss it is necessarily the result of his or her sin. Our own sins may well cause the suffering of others who are wounded by our cruel or insensitive actions or words.

The second explanation people often give, equally insupportable, is that those who suffer do not have enough faith, as if having enough faith somehow "earns" us God's miraculous intervention. The same examples will suffice to explode this theory. God commended Job for being "blameless and upright; he feared God and shunned evil" (Job 1:1), and later added a commendation for his faithfulness and integrity even under the assault of Satan. If Job didn't have enough faith to earn God's miraculous intervention, then you and I certainly don't. And what of Jesus on the cross? He too prayed for a miracle. Did He not have enough faith for God to reward Him by removing the cup of suffering He was about to face?

Besides, all of us recognize examples of the very opposite circumstances, which also disprove the theory about faith. We know evil people who don't suffer at all, a phenomenon that inspired the searching questions of Psalm 73:13: "Surely in vain have I kept my heart pure," the writer said, when he saw the wicked "always care-

free" and "increas[ing] in wealth" (v. 12). We see evil people who prosper.

No, the answer to the question, How could God let
this happen? is neither that somehow God has failed us
nor that we have somehow failed God. The disappointment with God shown in this question arises from two
false or precarious assumptions that we have made about
ourselves and about God. One is that God is obligated to
intervene in our world to accomplish a precise justice.
The other is that we really know what is good and what
is evil. Let's look at the first of these two assumptions: that
a good God must necessarily be always intervening to
keep everything in perfect balance in His world.

OUR FALSE ASSUMPTION THAT
GOD WILL OVERRULE OUR CHOICES

The classic statement of our dilemma is: Why does
God allow suffering and evil? Notice that the operative
word in this statement is "allow." God does not *cause* suffering and evil, but He does, obviously, allow it. The
question is, Why?

This is a legitimate question, and the answer reveals
something profound. It has to do with the very heart of
the human experiment. You see, God wanted to share
His own experience of life and joy with a being in His
creation. But to do that necessarily involved a genuine
freedom for that being. In order to share God's delight in
life, this creature would have to go beyond animal
instinct and actually *participate* in life through the ability
to make conscious choices.

Perhaps the most obvious example of this is the ability to love. Throughout the history of the human race,

love has been one of our highest pursuits. Kingdoms are won or lost for it. Fortunes are sacrificed for it. Lives are consumed by it. Our literature is obsessed with it. Almost no price seems too high to pay for it. But love, this high goal of ours, is impossible without free choices. No one really confuses an animal's instinctive drive to mate with genuine romance. You would not be satisfied with a "zombie" lover programmed by some internal drive to follow you around offering mechanical hugs and continually replaying a recorded message of eternal love. The wonder and joy of love is its voluntary nature, and the ever-present possibility that it could be withdrawn. There is no love without risk! Indeed, there is no joy, there is no life without risk. What takes our breath away is the realization that the person who commits to love us has freely chosen to do so, and need not have done it. The possibility that it wouldn't happen is what gives us the thrill when it does.

Choice is necessary in order to participate in and appreciate life. But with all free choice comes risk, for if we may freely choose what is good, we may also choose what is evil. This may be intentional, or it may be unintentional. We may *think* we are choosing the good when in fact we are choosing the evil. And choices, involving alternate destinies, will certainly have unforeseen consequences for us. Clearly, offering human creatures the possibility of free choice placed God's creation at enormous risk. The possibility of a sovereign God bringing good even out of our evil choices does not reduce the jeopardy in which we place His creation by those choices. Indeed, it opened the door for the possibility of terrible distortions and their consequent suffering. But it was a risk God obviously thought worth the taking, as it also offered the only possibility for that unfathomable delight in life that He wanted us to enjoy.

And we, along with the whole of the human race, have made some very bad choices, which have resulted in a bent or broken world where things do not always work the way they should, and where suffering and loss and evil are ever-present possibilities. Understand that God is not responsible for this. We are.

"But," you may protest, "why can't God do something about it? We're not saying He caused it. We may have brought it about. But why can't God intervene and set things right?" Ah, yes, our first assumption, that God is obligated to intervene with suffering in our world. But think about it; to intervene is to overrule and therefore to take away our free choices. Choice is meaningless if the consequences of our choices are constantly overruled, if there is no connection between our choices and what flows from them because of God's intervention.

Try to imagine a world in which God, like a compulsively overprotective or controlling parent, interfered with everything we did to make it come out His way instead of ours. Our choices would be meaningless in such a world. We would never really learn anything. And worst of all, we would never have the opportunity to experience the exhilaration of facing and overcoming the risks that give life its dynamic.

Why do people climb Mt. Everest? It is precisely the enormous risks involved that draw people to attempt an ascent of that awesome mountain. There would be absolutely no thrill in successfully climbing Everest if God simply eliminated every risk, countermanded every wrong choice, and guaranteed safety and success to everyone who made the attempt. No one would make the attempt! It would be as boring and unfulfilling an effort as one could possibly imagine if God were constantly suspending the law of gravity and holding off darkness and storms while we took a leisurely stroll to the top. Would we ever expend an effort if it weren't for the risks involved? Would we ever learn, would we ever dare if there were no real possibility of failure? Taking risks is part of being human.

If God intervened and negated the consequences of our actions, not only would it negate what it means for us to be human, but it would also destroy the possibility of our ever experiencing joy in accomplishment. In a very real way, the possibility of suffering is what makes us human.

Our False Assumption That
We Understand Good and Bad

The second precarious assumption implicit in our question about why God allows evil and suffering is that we really understand what is good and what is bad. It is a safe assumption that the reason God forbade Adam and Eve from sampling the fruit of the Tree of the Knowledge of Good and Evil was that it would tempt us to think we really knew what was good and what was bad, when in reality only God can know that. Is it bad for an innocent child to die young? It certainly seems that way to us. But how can we really know, this side of heaven? It is entirely possible that it looks very different from the other side. Is all pain irredeemable? Or is it possible that pain is an indispensable prerequisite for pleasure? Current medical theory suggests the two are intimately linked.

It is very presumptuous for us to think that we can know what God is doing through suffering and loss. I grew up in ranching country, and I often watched terrified livestock doing their best to avoid the trauma imposed by those who were simply looking out for their health and safety. Branding time was particularly traumatic. The animals were chased, roped, thrown to the ground, and immobilized, but the purpose was to mark them with some sort of identification so they could be cared for and to perform certain medical procedures that would protect them from disease and death. It didn't seem good to the animals, but it was the best thing that could happen to them.

Several years ago I got one of those phone calls every parent dreads, telling me that our son had severely fractured his leg while skiing. I met the bus when it arrived and transported him to the emergency room at the local hospital. The doctors decided to set the bone without anesthetic, since the break was clean through the tibia as well as the fibula, and they believed they needed the muscle taut enough to hold the two ends together. I wrapped my arms around my son and held him as his face turned white and his body shook convulsively with the pain while they pulled and twisted the injured leg in the first, rather violent step that would ultimately bring healing.

We live in a broken world, a world broken by our sin and our own errors in judgment, and that causes pain for ourselves and for others. But setting it right may also cause pain. It would have been quite understandable for my son to cry out, "Why are you doing this to me?" and to beg the physicians to stop causing him pain. But of course ending that pain would have been, on the whole, the worst thing we could have done to him. He needed that pain in order to heal.

Jesus cried out from the cross, in the words of Psalm 22:1, "My God, my God, why have you forsaken me? Why are you so far from saving me, so far from the words of my groaning?" David prophesied of His death by saying, "I am poured out like water, and all my bones are out of joint. My heart has turned to wax; it has melted away within me. My strength is dried up like a potsherd, and my tongue sticks to the roof of my mouth; you lay me in the dust of death" (vv. 14–15). Jesus was experiencing both the pain of a broken world and the pain that would be required to put it right. His suffering on the cross, intense and personal as it was, was part of a larger picture. It would bring Jesus Himself, along with all true believers, joy and even an ecstasy we cannot imagine. God's Word says the glory we will experience in His presence won't even be worth comparing to the suffering along the way.

In the end, we are called upon simply to trust. We don't always know the reasons. Maybe very seldom do we know the reasons. We are called upon to trust God when we cannot see or understand. "Why are you so far from saving me?" (Psalm 22:1) Jesus Himself cried out, when in fact the Father could not have been nearer. The pain was real and grievous, but it was a part of something much larger—a cosmic drama that would ultimately destroy pain and death altogether. These were things that we humans could not have seen. Indeed, Jesus Himself, in

His genuine humanness, could not, for the moment, see it. But God was working to accomplish His ultimate victory for the human race through that suffering.

We think we know what is good and what is bad, what ought to be and what ought not to be. But God assures us that He alone has the big picture, and He is fitting even the broken pieces of His world together to form something unimaginably great and good. He tells us Himself that this is true. One of the most remarkable statements in the entire Bible is found in Romans 8:28, where we read, "And we know that in all things God works for the good of those who love him, who have been called according to his purpose." In other words, regardless of how horrible or hopeless things may look to us, regardless of how much it hurts, God assures us that the very worst things can be—*will be,* for His children—instrumental in accomplishing the greatest and most delightful good things.

Chapter Two

FIRE ON THE

MOUNTAIN

Nehemiah 9:1–15

$\mathcal{W}$e live in a world constantly shaken by war and tragedy. Suffering and violence headline the evening news. Natural disasters like earthquakes, floods, and fires sweep down on people unawares. Criminals victimize a vulnerable public, seemingly with impunity. Selfish, evil people seem often to prosper, while good and loving people struggle through lives without tangible rewards. Death haunts every celebration and finally interrupts every life. In such a world, no one will blame us if we begin to lose heart and doubt other Christians' facile assurance that God is in control and everything will eventually turn out all right.

Yet that *is* what Christians believe. Is it just wishful thinking? Karl Marx, Friedrich Nietzsche, Sigmund Freud, and many of the other influential thinkers of this past century considered such ideas hopelessly naive—too good to be true. Religion, Freud said, was simply the imaginative projection of frightened and helpless humans, trying to create for themselves a place of refuge in a threatening world. Such men chose to believe instead that there is no God, that we are responsible for our own fate. But of course that conclusion brings with it far more serious and insuperable problems. A mindless universe offers no explanation for the origin of life. It fails to explain the consistency necessary for modern scientific exploration. Indeed, it destroys the very foundation of rational thought. It provides no basis for moral decisions. It cannot explain the fundamental human virtues of love and courage and self-sacrifice. And in the end it offers absolutely no hope for the future.

But if the alternatives have even less to offer, the question remains: How can Christians believe with confidence that things will work out for good, no matter how bad they seem? In the previous chapter we suggested that this conclusion was based on two fundamental assumptions: (1) that God is good and (2) that God is sovereign. We will explore the goodness of God later. Suffice it to say for the moment that if God is *not* good, then there is no hope—there could not be any conceivable hope if the Sovereign of the universe was not good. For Christians, of course, there is much more to support our conviction. In addition to what we may have heard from the prophets, or observed in a beautiful universe, or surmised from our own human ability to consider the good, we have the eloquent testimony of the life of our Lord Jesus Christ. In His compassion and sensitivity, which never compromises His sense of righteousness and justice, we see the good character of God revealed.

But here we want to look more closely at God's sovereignty. By sovereignty we mean simply that God is in control of every circumstance, every detail in the universe. God's Word says this should be evident to any thoughtful observer. "What may be known about God is plain to them, because God has made it plain to them. For since the creation of the world God's invisible qualities—his eternal power and divine nature—have been clearly seen, being understood from what has been made, so that men are without excuse" (Romans 1:19–20). We are responsible for this knowledge, the apostle explains, and the only way we can avoid it is if we purposely suppress it.

What is evident in the world around us is expressed particularly well in Psalm 135:5–7:

> I know that the Lord is great, that our Lord is greater than all gods. The Lord does whatever pleases him, in the heavens and on the earth, in the seas and all their depths. He makes clouds rise from the ends of the earth; he sends lightning with the rain and brings out the wind from his storehouses.

The Psalm goes on to enumerate obvious providential acts like His remarkable deliverance of His people from Egypt.

"Every animal of the forest is mine," Psalm 50:10–12 proclaims, "and the cattle on a thousand hills. I know every bird in the mountains, and the creatures of the field are mine ... for the world is mine, and all that is in it." All things belong to God, and He does what He pleases with them.

GOD'S INDEPENDENCE

When we say that God is in complete control of every detail in the universe, we are also saying that His actions are independent of any other will or power. You and I know nothing of this sort of freedom. All our decisions, and all the actions of our created world, are bound by a thousand other contingencies. At the beginning of his famous "Prelude," the English poet William Wordsworth rejoiced that he had escaped the confines of civilization and was now "free." He used the phrase "free as a bird to settle where I will." But of course, contrary to appearances, a bird is not really free at all. Naturalists will tell you that the bird is imprisoned by its instincts, its fears, its hungers, weather conditions, varying air pressures, the local food supply, the movement of predators, and a strangely compelling social harmony that keeps it from invading territory claimed by other birds. The bird isn't really free even though it appears to us to be.

Likewise for us, our freedom is restricted by physical and mental limitations; laws and their enforcement; social pressures; the restrictions of place and time and opportunity; physical laws such as gravity and inertia; the boundaries of our own genetic code, levels of wisdom, creativity, or skill; the cumulative influence of all our previous experiences; the presence or absence of other people; and uncounted other forces.

But God is not restricted by any of those elements. No one or no thing can stay His hand or keep Him from accomplishing His good will and pleasure. "I am God, and there is no other," He reminded us through Isaiah:

> I make known the end from the beginning, from ancient times, what is still to come. I say: My purpose will stand, and I will do all that I please. From the east I summon a bird of prey; from a far-off land, a man to fulfill my pur-

pose. What I have said, that will I bring about; what I have planned, that will I do. (46:9b–11)

And who, really, would challenge Him? Are there any other claimants to the throne? Isaiah again wrote,

> This is what the Lord says—Israel's King and Redeemer, the Lord Almighty: I am the first and I am the last; apart from me there is no God. Who then is like me? Let him proclaim it. Let him declare and lay out before me what has happened since I established my ancient people, and what is yet to come—yes, let him foretell what will come. (44:6–7)

How is it that God can lay out the future in such detail and with complete accuracy if He cannot control every detail of history?

> This is what the Lord says—your Redeemer, who formed you in the womb: I am the Lord, who has made all things, who alone stretched out the heavens, who spread out the earth by myself . . . who overthrows the learning of the wise and turns it into nonsense, who carries out the words of his servants and fulfills the predictions of his messengers. (44:24–26)

He went on to remind Israel how He had directed the Persian king, Cyrus, to accomplish His will and purpose in sending His people back.

OUR FALSE ASSURANCE OF OUR OWN INDEPENDENCE

Of course, today we are less likely to champion rival gods. Rather we are convinced that we ourselves hold our fate in our own hands. Such arrogance will one day be met with the challenge Job received when he presumed to question God's providence:

> Who is this that darkens my counsel with words without knowledge? Brace yourself like a man; I will question you, and you shall answer me. Where were you when I laid the earth's foundation? Tell me, if you understand. Who marked off its dimensions? Surely you know! Who stretched a measuring line across it? On what were its footings set, or who laid its cornerstone—while the morning stars sang together and all the angels shouted for joy? Who shut up the sea behind doors when it burst forth from the womb, when I made the clouds its garment and wrapped it in thick darkness, when I fixed limits for it and set its doors and bars in place, when I said, "This far you may come and no farther; here is where your proud waves halt"? Have you ever given orders to the morning, or shown the dawn its place, that it might take the earth by the edges and shake the wicked out of it? . . . Have the gates of death been shown to you? . . . Have you comprehended the vast expanses of the earth? Tell me, if you know all this. What is the way to the abode of light? And where does darkness reside? Can you take them to their places? Do you know the paths to their dwellings? Surely you know, for you were already born! You have lived so many years! . . . Can you bring forth the constellations in their seasons? . . . Do you know the laws of the heavens? Can you set up God's dominion over the earth? . . . Do you give the horse his strength? . . . Does the hawk take flight by your wisdom? . . . Will the one who contends with the Almighty correct him? . . . Would you discredit my justice? . . . Then adorn yourself with glory and splendor, and clothe yourself in honor and majesty. Unleash the fury of your wrath, . . . look at every proud man and humble him, crush the wicked where they

stand. Bury them all in the dust together; shroud their faces in the grave. Then I myself will admit to you that your own right hand can save you. (Job 38:2–13, 17–21, 32–33; 39:19, 26; 40:1, 8, 10–14)

There's not much left to say in response, is there?

Perhaps we still think we can question God. Job was wise enough and humble enough to realize he could not. "I know that you can do all things," Job responded in deep and genuine contrition. "No plan of yours can be thwarted. You asked, 'Who is this that obscures my counsel without knowledge?' Surely I spoke of things I did not understand, things too wonderful for me to know" (42:1–3).

This is what we mean when we speak of God's sovereignty. It encompasses not only the immense and beautiful choreography of the galaxies billions of miles into outer space, but, as He says in Matthew 10:29–30, He also knows when a sparrow falls, and He knows how many hairs are on your head. Ours is a God who attends to the minutest details of His creation in the accomplishment of His grand purpose.

Perhaps we, like Job, are chastened by this reminder of His sovereign power. But there remains the question with which we began. Why then is God not always kind to us? Why does He allow suffering and evil? That was precisely the question that haunted Job, of course, and for him it was not theoretical. It was incessantly, painfully real in the loss of all that was of value to him. God gives no answer to our question. But as we examine His actions throughout history, we begin to see that ours is not a soft, genial, benevolent god like that of eighteenth- and nineteenth-century Rationalism and Liberalism—a white-haired grandfather in the sky given to sighing and shaking his head at the exploits of rebel humans.

No, for better or for worse, ours is a God of fire on the mountain, a God who "breaks the bow and shatters the spear, [and who] burns the shields with fire" (Psalm 46:9). "Be still, and know that I am God," He says. "I will be exalted among the nations, I will be exalted in the earth" (v. 10).

We may think we would prefer a benign god who discreetly looked the other way when we shamed ourselves and who, like us, worshiped tolerance. But the fact is, we find ourselves with a God who *cares* absolutely about goodness and truth and justice. He will not be intimidated (as we so often are) by the howls and complaints of a self-indulgent, self-serving world demanding that we affirm its distortions and tolerate its whims. And He will not in the end, like a simpering, ineffective parent, let it have its own way. That's not the God we meet on the pages of Scripture or in our world. Like it or not, our God *acts* in history. He acts in perfect accordance with His own will and purpose, but the good news is He promises always to act in the ultimate best interests of His children.

And like it or not, this sovereignty is absolutely necessary. You and I must understand that if there exists even the tiniest exception to God's absolute control, no matter how insignificant or trivial it may seem, then God's rule is undone. You will, perhaps, remember the proverb: "For want of a nail, the shoe was lost; / For want of the shoe, the horse was lost; / For want of the horse, the rider was lost; / For want of the rider, the battle was lost; / For want of the battle, the kingdom was lost, / And all from the want of a horseshoe nail."

Suppose the man or woman God has groomed from

birth to negotiate peace between two warring nations—the one person who can recognize the nuances that characterize the two contending cultures—suppose this person has a tiny weak spot on a blood vessel in the brain and suffers a fatal stroke before the sides can be brought together? What happens in His world if God is not taking into consideration those few tiny cells in the wall of a blood vessel? World War I with its immeasurable suffering began as the result of the rash act of one out-of-control radical in the wrong place at the wrong time, and the whole world suffered. You see, every individual, every seemingly incidental circumstance has vast and endless possible implications. What if King Herod had had second thoughts a few days earlier and sent his assassins to Bethlehem before Joseph had a chance to escape with his stepson? You understand, the world is an integrated system. If anything, even the minutest detail of our lives, is beyond God's control, then He is simply not in control and cannot guarantee the outcome.

GOD'S CONTROL AND RESPONSIBILITY

But how, you ask, could He possibly have that sort of absolute control? The answer is simple. It is suggested to me by a simple text from Nehemiah 9:6: "You alone are the Lord. You made the heavens, even the highest heavens, and all their starry host, the earth and all that is on it, the seas and all that is in them. You give life to everything." How can anyone have that sort of absolute *authority?* No problem if you're the *Author.* That's where ultimate authority comes from.

You see, to understand God's ability to control even the minutest detail of His creation, we need only to recognize that He is *responsible* for every detail. Just as nothing appears in a book and nothing happens in a story that the author did not put there, so nothing, not any detail, appears in our universe and nothing happens here that God did not include on purpose. As we shall see, that even includes evil and suffering.

God did not *create* evil and suffering. They are not a *creation* at all. They are the distortion of something good that God created. But it is true, and it is no shocking new revelation, that God *did* consciously *allow* suffering and evil within His creation. We find them as early as the third chapter of Genesis, resulting from Adam and Eve's free choices, and we see them working at God's leave in the book of Job from which we quoted above. Whatever it is that God is doing within His creation, suffering and evil play a role—clearly a significant role. And God is not frustrated or intimidated by them. He recognizes them for what they are—serious and ugly distortions of His good creation—but nevertheless His will allowed them, and He has obviously incorporated them in the accomplishment of His grand design. This does not make them any less evil or painful. It simply impresses us with the scope of a sovereign goodness that may even embrace its own opposite, its own distortion, and use it to accomplish what is ultimately good and even perfect.

But we should never be surprised at God's sovereignty. No place ever exists in a book that was not first imagined in every detail by the author. No character ever exists in a book that the author did not create and place there. Those characters act, in a very real sense, freely. They make choices consistent with their character and opportunity. Yet no situation ever develops in a book that the author does not control. And no outcome is possible in a book that is contrary to the will of the author.

Genesis 1 reminds us that in the beginning there was nothing except God. He chose to bring all things into being. All things flow from Him. They do not exist or function apart from His continual investment of life and power. He brought the earth into being, along with every other planet and star, quasar and quark in the universe. All of them existed, first of all, only in His fertile imagination. He is the One who dreamed up "black holes" and decided to make them. Every living being on this planet was designed and brought into existence by Him. They do not have, they *cannot* have life in themselves. Every moment they are sustained by an extension of His life. Were He to withdraw, they would immediately cease to exist. As the story of life on this earth develops, it follows His script to the letter. Nothing *within* the story can change a word of the story, or even a punctuation mark. All are provided from the outside by the Author. And when the time comes to draw the story to its grand climax, who do you suppose will control every detail of the conclusion He has been approaching for all time?

In the ninth chapter of Nehemiah, the people finally realized that God had written a long and detailed story of which they were a part. Not only did He make everything that exists and comes to play in history, but He had continued to develop the story by calling Abram, by delivering his descendants from slavery in Egypt, by revealing His will to them in a covenant at Mt. Sinai, by continuing to love them even in their foolishness, by protecting them and directing their footsteps in the wilderness, by establishing them in the Promised Land,

and by disciplining them when they tried to ignore the God by whose leave they existed. Whatever it was that this Author had in mind for the culmination of His story, these people decided they wanted to be a part of it. So they chose the one intelligent option open to them. At the conclusion of that story, begun in Nehemiah 9, they entered into a covenant to cooperate with the God who was absolutely sovereign in the universe, and in whose hands rested every detail of their fate.

That seems to be a wise decision to make with regard to a God who is truly sovereign. And if in addition He is wholly and utterly good, then those who choose to walk with Him are clearly in for the most wonderful adventures, rife perhaps with risk and sometimes even genuine terror, but assured ultimately of success and of glory. What fool could resist the invitation?

Chapter Three

LIBERTY

OR DEATH

Genesis 2:15–17; 3:1–19

*I*t was a great idea, really, a plan to enable all eighteen cousins at our family reunion to create their own T-shirt designs. Brightly colored pink and teal and blue shirts were spread out on floors and benches and tables around a large recreation room. Each child received several tubes of thick, pasty T-shirt paint with which to create his or her own masterpiece. I watched one niece for some time. She worked particularly diligently for more than an hour, drawing elaborate pictures and carefully lettering her shirt with a message about the family. When it was finally complete, she stepped back to admire her handiwork. And at that precise moment another young cousin, preoccupied with his own world, strolled mindlessly across her canvas, leaving several smeared tennis shoe prints where a moment before had been a design of some particular beauty. Understandably, she burst into tears.

In that moment of horror and frustration and tears, I

think my niece must have experienced something similar to God's reaction to Adam and Eve's desecration of His masterpiece in the Garden of Eden, and how He must feel when we do the same. Of course God saw it coming, and He is not helpless to do anything about it, but the sense of violation must be similar. We've been talking about God's incredible promise to work everything out for good in our world, and in the previous chapter we spoke of His sovereign control of the universe. I hope you were encouraged by the majesty and the magnificence of God's sovereignty. I think we might be persuaded that this sovereign God is weaving, or at least *could* weave, every circumstance of life into a perfect tapestry, *if* we could be persuaded that He really does control everything. But doesn't it seem that free-wheeling, self-absorbed, and unpredictable human beings are the potential "wrench in the works" of His creation, more likely than not to leave our distorted footprints across the landscape of Eden?

THE PROBLEM OF FREE WILL

The problem seems to lie in what we would consider to be God's questionable decision to create a being capable of exercising what we have generally called "free will." Granting that God is more than capable of suppressing that free will if He chooses, and doing whatever He desires, God seems to have voluntarily bound His own sovereignty with this creature that makes up its own mind about what to do or acts without exercising its mind at all. How can God guarantee a good outcome to everything that happens in the world when this "loose cannon" on deck has slipped its moorings and is now spinning and crashing out of control with every heave of the ship? Human freedom seems to us the Achilles' heel, the one vulnerable spot in God's creation. Whatever He has planned, it appears to us that we are always capable of "messing it up," or at least of "messing up" our own lives and usually a number of others along with ourselves.

This certainly appears to be the issue in the account of creation from the book of Genesis. Paradise was perfect until human beings freely chose to disobey God. From that point on, things went from bad to worse. Is it really possible for God to make a carte blanche promise to bring everything together for good, if we can continually interfere and change the course of history? It would seem to us that human freedom would *always* be a challenge to God's sovereignty. So what's He going to do about it? Can He control His universe without suppressing human freedom? Will suppression of freedom be necessary in heaven? How will this work?

The discussion about the nature and effects of human freedom has gone on for a long time, but it is easy for us to misunderstand the issues. If we are to understand how God intends to make everything work together for good for His children, we must understand what the real issue is concerning human freedom. And it's not what most of us think.

The problem is that however you frame a question, you have already prejudiced the answer. The framing of the question determines the sort of answers received. Pollsters know that. We see it constantly in political surveys. So with the question of human freedom. In the secular, scientific, and psychological world, the question is: Is Mankind free or determined? In other words, are we only slaves of the natural influences of our environment, or can human nature rise above the environment? Is biology destiny? Are we programmed by our DNA and all the other biological and environmental factors in our lives to act in a certain way, or can we make choices that override our environment and biology? The question has far-reaching implications for whether we are held accountable for our actions, including criminal behavior and sexual preferences. Are we responsible for this or not? That's the discussion that arises from the question as the secular scientific world places it before us.

The philosophical and theological discussion, however, has generally centered on a different question: Does God's sovereignty negate mankind's freedom? This question raises an entirely different set of issues. It's the question we have just been discussing. If humans are capable of choosing their own direction and destiny freely, then this must restrict God's sovereignty. If on the other hand God controls every detail of the universe, then He must also control the choices and actions of every individual human. But these two options have far-reaching and disquieting implications as well. A world that God does not control is a terrifying place indeed, and no promises can be made about the outcome. On the other hand, if He controls every detail, then He appears to be responsible for the evil and suffering that surround us in our world. That conclusion would end all hope.

THE QUESTION OF FREEDOM

I would like to suggest, however, that neither of these approaches frames the question properly. In the Bible, the question is not, Is mankind free or determined? nor is it,

Does God's sovereignty negate mankind's freedom? In the Bible, the question is, Are you a slave to sin or are you a slave to God? That's the only issue as the Bible sees it. Quite frankly, the Bible does not seem to consider questions of human freedom or of the apparent conflict between God's sovereignty and our free will to be particularly relevant. We simply do not have pure freedom. Only God has that. What we have is the freedom to choose our master. Paul goes on about this at some length in Romans 6:

> Don't you know that when you offer yourselves to someone to obey him as slaves, you are slaves to the one whom you obey—whether you are slaves to sin, which leads to death, or to obedience, which leads to righteousness? But thanks be to God that, though you used to be slaves to sin, . . . you have been set free from sin and have become slaves to righteousness. (Romans 6:16–18)

Those are the two possibilities from a biblical standpoint. Now listen carefully to what he says next, for it forms the heart of what we want to say about true freedom:

> [Let me] put this in human terms [for you] . . . Just as you used to offer the parts of your body in slavery to impurity and to ever-increasing wickedness, so now offer them in slavery to righteousness leading to holiness. When you were slaves to sin, you were free from the control of righteousness. What benefit did you reap at that time from the things you are now ashamed of? Those things result in death! But now that you have been set free from sin [through the blood of Jesus Christ] and have become slaves to God, the benefit you reap leads to holiness, and the result is eternal life. (Romans 6:19–22)

You see, the Bible doesn't even consider the question of whether you are free from the controlling influence of both sin and God. That kind of autonomous freedom belongs to God alone. We have a choice, but it is not a choice to be free of any outside influence. It is a choice to submit to God's influence or to fall into a devastating slavery to sin. If our wills, the Bible tells us, are not submitted to God, they *will* be submitted to sin. If that is the case, we *will* be compelled to follow our own fallen desires. And that will be no freedom. That will be the worst kind of slavery we can imagine.

Let's go back for a moment to the Garden of Eden. Often we talk as if Adam and Eve's freedom lay in their ability to stand back and exercise their free will to choose between competing options which they might pursue. But if we look more closely, we see that God only offered them one option. He showed them which way freedom lay. Freedom lay in embracing the world as God had made it. For their part, they could take it or leave it. As long as they walked in obedience to Him, they would be free to enjoy a place in His universe. When they turned from it, they would encounter inevitable Death. But of course, Death is not an option for our lives. Death is the end of all options. Adam and Eve had only one option. It was freedom or nothing. Liberty or Death! The liberty to be human if they obeyed God, or death if they did not. That's it. You and I have the same singular option. It is for us also Freedom or Nothing. Freedom to enjoy everything God wants to give us, or the loss of everything.

THE DEFINITION OF TRUE FREEDOM

The term "free will" is probably misleading. It

implies some sort of neutrality, a capacity for utter self-determination. But only God is capable of self-determination. It is a quality of sovereignty, and if we think we are candidates for sovereignty, we have fallen for Satan's original temptation. No, what Adam and Eve had was the possibility of embracing the freedom to be human. They could choose or reject freedom; that was their singular option. If they rejected it, they were left with nothing but the ashes of Eden.

Is it not freedom that all mankind has sought so passionately throughout the entire scope of human history? But, you see, freedom has always been there for the taking! It has been right in front of every person who has ever lived. It lies for us where it lay for Adam and for Eve. "You are free," God said, free to enjoy all the fruits of the Garden, free to enjoy what it is to be human, if you simply continue to do My will. "But you must not eat from the tree of the knowledge of good and evil"; you must not attempt to stand on some neutral pinnacle above good and evil where all options are equally available to you, "for when you eat [that fruit] you will surely die" (Genesis 2:17). Freedom and life and joy are yours in Me, God says. Everything else is Death. *Everything* else is Death.

You see, the problem as Scripture sees it is not whether we are determined or free. The Bible is perfectly clear that humans are indeed free agents. We are not determined. Whatever the influences on our lives, we are responsible for our choices. God's Word is very clear about that. That is our dignity and our nobility.

Nor does Scripture see a problem with God's sovereignty disallowing our freedom. On the contrary, as I hope you are beginning to see, God's sovereignty creates our freedom and offers it to us in this garden of delights. *The threat to our freedom is not God's sovereignty; it is our sin.* That is a tremendously important insight. Under God's sovereignty, Adam and Eve were truly free. It was possible for them to be fully human and to remain free from sin. After the Fall, after they had rejected God's authority in their lives, after turning away from Him, their freedom was lost, and it was no longer possible for them not to sin. It would take a special act of God's sovereignty through the grace of Jesus Christ to restore their lost freedom.

Which way, then, does freedom lie for us? Not, certainly, in the way the world proclaims. Freedom does not lie in the way of "doing whatever we want." It was in choosing *that* way that we *lost* our freedom. What an astonishing feat Satan has accomplished in convincing us that freedom lies in exactly the opposite direction from where it really lies. To choose to do whatever we want to do is to choose an utter slavery to our bodily appetites and desires. We were made in the image of God, in His likeness. True freedom then has to consist in conforming to His will and His desire, for we are free only when we are being and doing precisely what we were created to be and to do. Anything less than this is not freedom. It is Death.

One example of this might be an automobile engine. When it is operating as it is designed to operate, it is a thing of beauty and power. As the engine rotates, a cam lifts and closes valves precisely, and those valves allow a precise mixture of fuel and oxygen from the carburetor to enter the cylinder. As the piston rises, this mixture of fuel is compressed and then ignited by a spark from the spark plug at precisely the right moment. The resulting explosion drives the piston down with great force, creating the power by which the driveshaft is rotated and power is ultimately transferred to the wheels. All that happens with great precision. The adventurer behind the wheel, guiding his or her sports machine to its destination, seems to fly effortlessly around the winding curves. What a picture of freedom this is!

But suppose something in that engine does what it was *not* designed to do. Suppose a valve jams or a rod penetrates a cylinder wall—what becomes of this picture of freedom? You see, there is no tolerance here. It does what it was designed to do, or it dies. You and I do what we were designed to do, or we die.

With a person, the picture becomes even clearer. A sprinter like the late Florence Griffith-Joyner looks the picture of grace and beauty as she runs, but this freedom does not come from doing whatever she feels like doing. It comes from submitting her body to the precise exercises required to produce a runner. Itzhak Perlmann's fingers fly over the strings of his violin, creating exquisitely beautiful music, but those fingers have been trained by rigorous discipline. Artists are free to draw, musicians to play, and athletes to compete because they have submitted to the necessary disciplines of their art. All true freedoms grow from submission to the rules.

For us also, freedom is *not* the possibility of making any choice we may possibly desire. Rather, we choose freedom when we choose to conform our actions and behavior to the way they ought to be. Made in God's image, we have the possibility of conforming to the total character of God, in which case we would be totally free to be and to do and to accomplish and to enjoy every-thing it's possible for a human to be and to do and to enjoy. To choose *not* to conform to God's character, how-ever, can mean nothing but death, for it means to choose not to be human. The eagle's freedom to soar comes from his utter conformity to being an eagle. Should he choose to be a stone, or even a fish, it would mean the death of the eagle. True human freedom describes only the person who is totally "in sync" with God's will, made in His image, conformed to that image, doing what he or she was designed to do.

THE WRONG IDEA OF FREEDOM

The most incredibly beautiful and powerful and free person who has ever lived is Jesus Christ. He was enslaved to nothing. He demonstrated a power over Himself and over creation that startled and awed those who saw Him. He had the power to deal gracefully and boldly with any situation that ever confronted Him. He never lost control. He was never frustrated in His ability to do whatever He desired. He had the ability to laugh and love and grieve and challenge whenever it was appropriate. But where did His remarkable human free-dom come from? He spelled it out for us in no uncertain terms. He said, "I always do what pleases him" (John 8:29). I *always* do what I was created to do.

You see, we've had it all backward. We are decidedly *not* free in the sense of being autonomous, free to do whatever we choose. Our being, our life, our very ability to consider and choose come from God. We are utterly dependent on Him. However, neither are we automa-tons. We can only experience and enjoy life if our choices are real. But our choice is not a "free" choice between competing options. It is a choice to be free—or, in the absence of freedom, to die. Liberty or death! Patrick Henry had something else in mind, but he spoke a profound truth. In the Garden of Eden God too said I'll give you liberty or death. Each of us will either be a slave to God or a slave to sin, a slave to God's desires or a slave to our own fallen appetites. The former choice brings with it an utter and complete freedom to be human in the fullest and most extraordinary way, and ultimately it leads to Life. The latter choice leads to a complete breakdown of our humanness and ultimately to Death.

This should give us a wholly new perspective on human freedom. It is not the freedom to do whatever we want. It is the freedom to be wholly and wonderfully human, a freedom that comes, quite obviously now I hope, from conforming our behavior to the will and character of the God who made us in His likeness. That's our choice. You want freedom? You may have it by embracing the whole of the person and the character of God.

Understanding now what freedom really means, we want to return to our opening concern about whether human freedom might not intervene, in some way, with the accomplishment of God's perfect purposes. But this new knowledge has changed our perspective. Whether we choose, as Paul spelled out in Romans 6, to submit our lives to the Lord, or to let them fall into slavery to our own desires, in the end, neither of these options is a threat to the accomplishment of God's divine purpose. Indeed, as you may see now that we have defined freedom as conformity to the will of God, our true freedom, far from being a threat to God's plan, is rather an instrument in the accomplishment of His plan. The promise of Romans 8:28 is to those who have chosen to submit their will to God's and who have become, as a result, an integral part of His divine plan. To these people God restores, through the power of His divine grace, their true freedom, lost in their original rebellion against God. Jesus' promise in John 8:34, 36 is "Everyone who sins is a slave to sin. . . . So if the Son sets you free, you will be free indeed."

It is a joyous and remarkable freedom. The person who is completely conformed to the will of God has an entire universe of possibilities before him. Can you even imagine it? According to 1 Corinthians 3:21–22, "All things are yours, whether . . . the world or life or death or the present or the future—all are yours, [why? because] you are of Christ, and Christ is of God." The whole thing is in His hands. Everything is yours if you are in His hands. "The more communion with God fills our life, the more free our life becomes," Dutch theologian G. C. Berkouwer explained.[1] So the truly free human being is no threat to God's sovereignty whatsoever. He or she fits in perfectly. As for those who have rejected God's offer of freedom, they can be no threat because they can no longer act freely. They have become entirely predictable slaves marching in lockstep toward death. They have opted out of God's plan, out of any blessing or any possible good, and are therefore sovereignly excluded from the accomplishment of God's good things. They have rejected freedom, but God still controls their fading universe absolutely.

If you understand what we have said about the

nature of true freedom, you will see that it is a mistake—more than a mistake, it is a gross distortion—to place God's sovereignty and our freedom in opposition to each other, as if the two are competing for supremacy. Too often we act as if one must win and the other lose. We think, *If I give way to God, I will have conceded my freedom.* But, we must see, it is exactly the opposite. In giving way to God we gain our freedom. If we lose, it is not because God has won, but because in our rebellion against Him, we have chosen to discard our freedom. God's desire is that we might both win, and we win most spectacularly when our wills respond in glorious concert with His—when we join in the dance. A precision flying team is the very image of freedom and beauty, making great loops and swirls against the sky. But it depends utterly on following the will of the leader and obeying the laws of aerodynamics. We have been invited to be partners in a great and graceful dance in which He leads and we follow. This, and this alone, is liberty. All else is death. Our joy is that the Lord of the Dance controls all things for our good!

NOTE

1. G. C. Berkouwer, *Man: The Image of God* (Grand Rapids: Eerdmans, 1962), 322.

Section Two

THE PROMISE

Chapter Four

WITHOUT

EXCEPTION

Romans 8:28;
Philippians 4:4–7

*D*o you ever wish your life had been different? Suppose, for example, that you were blessed with an exquisite physical beauty, or maybe an enviable athleticism. Suppose you had the capacity to be a brilliant scholar or an incredible artist or musician. Suppose the circumstances that have shaped you had been different. Suppose your parents had been far more creative, compassionate, and wise. Suppose you had chosen a different career path, one that by now would have given you opportunities for wealth and success and exotic opportunities to travel and experience the world.

Of course, there are "what ifs" on the other side, also. What if you had been born with a devastating physical condition that left you severely handicapped? What if you were falsely accused of some heinous crime? What if some disaster had destroyed your home and family? What if the person you loved and respected more than anyone in the world betrayed you? Life holds a lot of "what ifs," for better or for worse.

Most of us spend entirely too much time and energy wishing things were different. In the first place, most of the things we lament cannot be changed. Of course I am not suggesting that we passively allow life to happen without making any plans or striving toward any goals. I am simply saying that many givens in our lives are beyond our control, and we waste a lot of our energy wishing things were different.

But the second reason is far more fascinating and compelling. God's Word suggests that every single thing that has happened in our lives, through God's providence, contributes precisely what we need to be shaped into the persons who can most perfectly reflect and take delight in God's glory! That is at the heart of the promise of Romans 8:28, "And we know that in all things God works for the good of those who love him, who have been called according to his purpose." *In all things:* in the color of your hair and the shape of your body, in the particular skills and interests that characterize you, in the people who have shaped your life for better or for worse along the way, in the particular opportunities and experiences that are unique to you, and yes, even in the failures and the disappointments that have marked your life to date. In and through all these things, God is working to shape you into a creature of exquisite glory!

Do you wonder if I am overstating the case? How can I be confident of such a sweeping generalization? I don't know the details of your life. How can I say this? I'll tell you how: because God's Word says, first of all, "We know." It doesn't say, "We *hope* this might be true," or

"We *think* maybe, if the circumstances are right." It says, "We *know.*" We know that all things work together for the good of those who love God!

And you might ask, How do we know this? We know it *because God is sovereign and He has promised.* Earlier we looked at what it means for God to be sovereign, and we found a very wonderful thing. We found God to be in absolute control of every detail of the universe. No detail, no matter how apparently small or insignificant (like the hairs on our head or the fall of a sparrow), escapes His attention; and nothing, not even the hostile rebellion of a man or an angel, can stay His hand from accomplishing His perfect will. "I am God, and there is no other," He says. "I am God, and there is none like me. I make known the end from the beginning . . ." Do you doubt His control? "I make known the end from the beginning, from ancient times, what is still to come. I say: My purpose will stand, and I will do all that I please" (Isaiah 46:9–10). And what pleases God is to work everything in your life to the accomplishment of a good end.

The sovereign Lord and Creator of the universe is our Shepherd, David tells us in Psalm 23, and we are the sheep of His pasture. He walks with us through every detail of our lives, caring for our daily needs, protecting us from unnecessary harm, teaching us to trust Him, even leading us through the very portals of death itself, on our way to the great feast He has prepared for His beloved.

GOD OF THE DETAILS

We are confident that nothing in our lives is for naught, because the God who created us to share His glory and delight has control of every detail of our lives. That is a fundamental truth on which we can build everything else. "We know that in *all things* God works for the good of those who love him." The word translated "all things" is the Greek word that can be transliterated *panta*, which simply means everything—without exception. A little further on in Romans 11, Paul uses the same word in uttering one of his great doxologies, "For from him and through him and to him are *all things!*" (v. 36). *Panta!* And 1 Corinthians 8:6 speaks of God the Father "from whom *all things* came." Thus when the word *panta* is used in this promise concerning God working for good in our lives, it includes absolutely everything that ever happens in our lives, without exception. That's a remarkable promise. *Absolutely everything that ever happens in your life as a believer contributes in some substantial way to God's good and perfect plan for your life.* Do you believe it? My goal is to help that astonishing truth begin to soak in and to begin to suggest the tremendous difference it should make in our lives.

One of the primary reasons God gave us the Scriptures of the Old and New Testaments was to let us see His remarkable promises working themselves out in the lives of ordinary people. There we see Him at work not only in the good things that happen to people, but very much at work in the bad things as well. In the history of God's people, we see Him accomplishing His good purposes not only in good and wise leadership, say of a prophet like Samuel, but also in the deplorable, self-indulgent, even promiscuous behavior of the judge Samson.

After Israel had enjoyed the courageous and inspired leadership of David and Solomon, Rehoboam's insensitivity led to Israel's devastating division. Yet when noble and courageous men tried to intervene, God stopped them with these words: "Do not go up to fight against your brothers ... *for this is my doing*" (1 Kings 12:24). God was at work, accomplishing His will and purpose through the foolish decisions of the man in leadership at the time.

GOD OF ALL CIRCUMSTANCES

During times too numerous to mention God blessed His people with prosperity and protection, but at other times He awakened them to their peril and passivity with exposure to great trials and suffering. Even among Christ's followers, while God offered Peter miraculous protection and deliverance from prison, Peter's friend Stephen was denied that protection, instead suffering persecution and death. Although God preserved a powerful witness in Peter, it was the persecution of Stephen, the Bible tells us, that forced the early believers to leave their comfort behind and scatter to other cities where they continued to bear witness to the good news of the risen Christ, and the church began to spread like wildfire. Persecution is a terrible thing, but God was using that persecution in Stephen's life to accomplish something good. Meanwhile he had prepared a place of astonishing glory for Stephen, which He let him see just when things had gotten to their worst. God was working for good in the bad things as well as in the good things.

And God did not just work in dramatic things either, but in everyday things, like people's marriages. Priscilla and Aquila in the early church apparently had a wonderfully strong and mutually respectful marriage, which God used to build up the church and help train individual leaders. But you will remember that in the Old Testament He used Hosea's terrible marriage to reassure His people of His faithfulness in the face of our unfaithfulness. What is God doing to shape you right now in your marriage or in your closest personal relationships? How might God be at work in the unfair treatment you might be receiving right now or in some hardship or pain you are experiencing? God promises that He is indeed working in all these things to accomplish His good and perfect will and purpose in your life.

But when God assures us that He is working for good in "all things," He is talking about more than simply good and bad. God works in big things as well as little things. His hand was strikingly evident in the series of horrendous plagues that struck Egypt and finally motivated the Pharaoh to set God's people free. The Nile River turned to blood; frogs, gnats, flies, and locusts infested the nation; disease killed much of their livestock, while festering boils plagued most of the population; a tremendous hailstorm devastated the crops; and finally darkness and death invaded even the household of the king. God was at work in earth-shattering events. But God is not only at work in the fate of empires. One of His great demonstrations of power grew out of a small boy's simple generosity in sharing his handful of loaves and fishes to feed a multitude! Is it possible that your invitation to share coffee or a Thanksgiving meal may have implications of greater significance even than some national event? Mao Tse-tung was turned away from a mission school in his youth and went on to outlaw Christianity in the largest nation in the world. Might some small kindness not have changed the course of history?

God works in good things and bad, big things and little; He works in important things as well as the seemingly incidental. The people who were opposing the rebuilding of the temple by the Jews who had returned from exile wrote a formal letter to King Darius requesting official intervention from the head of the Persian Empire. This diplomatic exchange was met by an official search of the records, which revealed the decree of an earlier and even greater King Cyrus in support of the temple project (Ezra 5–6). The result was a royal measure of support that carried the project to completion in record time—a very important event in the life of Israel!

But in another time and place a seemingly incidental occurrence involving a humble and unknown foreign maiden led to the establishment of the royal line of David in Bethlehem. It is in the story of Ruth, who had returned to Israel with her widowed mother-in-law. In their poverty Ruth had offered to go glean in the fields —picking up leftover grain behind the harvesters. "As it turned out," the text tells us rather incidentally, "she found herself working in a field belonging to Boaz" (Ruth 2:3). It appeared to be incidental, but that quaint little coincidence led to her marriage and the birth of her son, who became the grandfather of the great King David who brought Israel to her "Golden Age."

God works through things that are done on purpose, as well as things that just seem to happen by chance. Nehemiah, an exiled Jew whose organizational and administrative skills had landed him a position in the court of the Persian king Artaxerxes, and later got him appointed governor of Israel, used his considerable talents to redesign and rebuild the walls of the city of

Jerusalem, organizing a massive workforce in the accomplishment of that purpose. God worked through his skills and his determined pursuit of this particular goal to accomplish a very significant step in the reorganization of His people. But during the reign of Artaxerxes' father, a series of random events involving a young Jewish girl named Esther uncover the hidden hand of God in the events of our daily lives. We shall explore that story in the next chapter.

Good and bad, big and little, important and incidental, purposeful and apparently random—God is at work in *all things* to accomplish good for His children. Sometimes His hand is very apparent, as in the spectacular pillar of fire in the wilderness guiding and protecting His people. Sometimes it is hidden, as when Elisha and his servant were protected by an army of angels in flaming chariots that no one could see until God opened their eyes.

GOD'S WORK THROUGH OUR FAILURES

It may seem obvious that God works through our successes, like that of Joshua and the army that crossed the Jordan River with him to conquer the Promised Land. But it is also worth noting that their failure to rally behind Moses' leadership forty years earlier led to a crucial time of toughening and consolidation for this ragtag group of runaway slaves as they struggled to survive their wilderness exile. God used that failure in a remarkable way to give the Jews an identity that sustains them to this day.

Not only did God work through the tremendous success of the noble Daniel who lived so faithfully, but He also used Peter's humiliating failure in denying Christ to shape him into a humble and faithful and effective servant.

As the early church grew, the young Timothy consistently pleased everyone by his perseverance and maturity. It was easy to see how God might use this young man's successes. But don't forget the youthful John Mark who couldn't handle the rigors of the road with Paul and Barnabas. His failure to continue with them upset Paul so much that he and Barnabas split up their effective mission team. But the end result was that while Barnabas encouraged his nephew John Mark to try again, Paul recruited another effective missionary in Silas. Not only did John Mark succeed this time, but he went on to become one of Paul's favorite and most trusted colleagues, eventually writing the gospel of Mark. God does not work only through our successes. He may accomplish His greatest work through our failures.

The fact is, as Romans 8:28 states so powerfully, nothing at all is lost in God's economy. He uses everything that has shaped us in the past, everything that is happening in our lives at this very moment, and everything that still waits in store for us in the future. I am impressed by the way in which God used everything in Moses' life to build him into a unique and effective servant leader. Born the son of slaves, he was always concerned for justice and sensitive to the vulnerability of the lowest people in society. Raised in the royal court, he understood politics and power and was at ease in the presence of royalty. An early career in the military in Egypt taught him leadership skills, whereas a lengthy stint as a fugitive, making a living herding sheep in the wilderness, taught him invaluable survival skills and enabled him later to orient across a trackless wilderness with the survival of his people depending upon him.

God used everything in Moses' life to shape him for his particular calling.

Many in our day will testify to the same economy in their own lives. Dr. Paul Brand has written of his early apprenticeship in carpentry, which seemed a waste of time when he instead became a surgeon. But God used those skills and interests to enable him to develop a shop where recovering leprosy patients could learn a trade. God, in His economy, doesn't waste anything in our lives.

C. S. Lewis's outspoken Christian critique of his colleagues apparently cost him a professorship at Oxford University. He worked for twenty-nine years as a tutor, correcting all his own papers, carrying extra classes, working one-on-one with a myriad of students at low pay until finally, late in his career, Cambridge University offered him a full professorship. But Lewis credits that constant and demanding interaction with students and their questions as one of the most influential forces in helping him become such an effective communicator. God used what was really unfair and often a burden to make him the person who was most effective at his calling.

Charles Colson found the experience of his public humiliation during the Watergate crisis to be not only the experience that brought him to Christ, but his subsequent imprisonment motivated his establishment of the tremendously effective Prison Fellowship ministry. Colson was suffering the consequences of his own sin. Aleksandr Solzhenitsyn suffered the consequences of other people's sin. Yet that great Russian author could say, "Bless you, prison, for having been in my life!" after spending time in the Soviet gulag. He concluded that this was the most important experience in his life. It shaped who he became and what he was able to contribute in his world-changing literary career.

GOD'S PRESENCE IN THE HARD TIMES

Can you believe that God uses *all things* to accomplish His good purposes in your life? The apostle Paul could believe it, which is why he exhorted believers in Philippians 4:6 not to "be anxious about anything," and to thank God for "everything" that takes place. You see, the person who really understands that God has not overlooked even the most minor detail, but is working *everything* out in the long run for our good, will be overwhelmed with genuine gratitude to God for everything that happens in his life.

After my sister lost her husband to a brain tumor at age thirty-four, she confessed how grateful she was to have been allowed the intense sense of God's tangible presence upholding her during that tragedy. "I would never choose that course, nor would I wish it on anyone else," she said. "And yet there has never been a time in my life when I have been more aware of God's presence and His love." As painful and traumatic as was the loss of her husband, it gave her an opportunity to glimpse God's glory.

Paul spelled out for us in Philippians some of the ways in which this knowledge of God's use of all things for our good might affect us. He suggested that it may give us the ability to take delight in all things. Most of us know people who are able to express their delight in life, in spite of all the painful and disappointing things that happen. But this can only be true if we understand that God is working all things together for good in our lives.

Second, his gratitude to God for His sovereign care gave him the freedom to be gracious toward others. When you know God is using even the worst intentional evil directed against you to accomplish something wonderful in your life, you can afford to be gracious.

Third, his awareness that the Lord was using *all things* to prepare for the day of His return and His establishment of an unimaginable paradise gave Paul an incredible and tenacious confidence in the future. If you know that everything in your life is in God's hands, and that all things are working to a good end, then you can have an enormous confidence in what's still to come.

And finally, Paul realized that such an awareness of the hand of God in *all things* gave him a tremendous freedom from anxiety and worry. If you and I are spending our time and our energy worrying about what's taking place in our lives, it's because we haven't really claimed this promise from Romans 8:28. Yes, we can make decisions that cause us great pain. But even there God says He will use that to make us into the most complete and whole and perfect persons we can ever imagine. The person who knows that God uses absolutely everything to accomplish His good purposes in our lives will finally experience that "peace of God, which transcends all understanding" (Philippians 4:7).

Chapter Five

GOD'S

TAPESTRY

The year was 483 B.C. and the Persian Empire was at its peak, ruling a vast kingdom that stretched from the Indus River in today's Pakistan north of India; across what are now Afghanistan, Iran, and Iraq; on around the Fertile Crescent through Syria, Jordan, and Israel; then across the Suez and down through Egypt and into Sudan. King Xerxes' father, Darius, had built a lavish capital at Persepolis, as well as a winter palace at Susa, and had even dug a canal between the Nile River and the Red Sea. Vast networks of roads made it possible for him to move his armies around the empire with remarkable efficiency. One such road ran 1,500 miles from Susa, near the Persian Gulf, all the way across Asia Minor to Sardis, near the Aegean. Xerxes, meanwhile, was amassing a powerful navy in anticipation of a simultaneous land and sea attack on the small but attractive Greek city-states, an attack that would be immortalized at places like Thermopylae and Salamis in the great Persian Wars.

Within this wealthy and powerful empire lived an obscure people who had once occupied one tiny corner of the land before being displaced by the Babylonians. They had no status in the empire, but their obstinate refusal to conform had preserved their identity as a people, while stirring significant resentment against them.

As the book of Esther opens, we learn that King Xerxes has just called for a great banquet for his nobles in celebration of his "vast wealth" and "the splendor and glory of his majesty" (1:4). The feast took place in the citadel in Susa, amidst a lavish setting of blue and white linens attached to marble pillars by silver rings, and flanking "couches of gold and silver on a mosaic pavement of porphyry, marble, mother-of-pearl and other costly stones" (v. 6).

At the height of the festivities, and perhaps a bit intoxicated both by an excess of wine and by too great acclaim, the king decided to show off his wife, the queen, identified here by what is possibly a pet name, Vashti, meaning "beloved" or "the desired one." The queen, apparently not wishing to be ogled by her husband's inebriated guests, refused to come, but she had no rights over against her husband's, and she was subsequently deposed. Later, when the king was having second thoughts about his rash decision (2:1), his officials persuaded him to host a nationwide beauty pageant to select an alternate queen. Thus it was that Esther, a young orphaned Jewish girl of remarkable beauty, in exile from her own nation, became queen of the most powerful empire in the world.

Esther had been raised by a cousin who went by the name of Mordecai, a name derived from the Babylonian deity Marduk. It is possible that he was the accountant Mardukaya, mentioned in a cuneiform tablet, who served in Susa during the early years of Xerxes' reign. In any case, he advised Esther not to reveal her nationality. As he served at the king's gate, he kept in regular contact with his adopted daughter in the palace. At one point, Mordecai overheard plans to assassinate the king, but he foiled the plot by reporting it to Esther.

Among the officers in the king's court was an extremely vain, self-aggrandizing man by the name of Haman who had risen to a position of considerable influence in the kingdom, and who received obeisance from everyone except Mordecai, who refused to honor him. Haman became so obsessed with Mordecai's affront that he resolved to have him exterminated along with all of his people. Through subterfuge and flattery he convinced the king to give him permission to destroy these anonymous rebels who were such a threat to the empire, and the king issued an irreversible decree to that end. A date was set for the massacre by throwing dice to determine the most propitious day for this event, and the fate of Haman's enemies seemed assured. As one would imagine, this threw the entire Jewish community into dread and dismay.

Mordecai urged Esther to plead their cause with the king. Esther, knowing the history that brought her to the throne, was well aware that she had no rights with the king. She was fearful of approaching him with her request, but ultimately she accepted the challenge.

Haman, meanwhile, was so consumed with Mordecai's behavior that he decided he couldn't wait, and he had a gallows built with the intention of asking the king's permission to have his enemy hanged. The night before he was going to the king with this request, however, the king couldn't get to sleep and finally called a secretary to read to him. Reading in the annals of his reign, they came across the account of Mordecai's uncovering of the plot against the king. Xerxes realized he had never suitably rewarded Mordecai for saving the king's life.

In the morning Haman came early to the king's court to be first in line with his petition for Mordecai's execution. The king, however, spoke first and asked Haman's advice on how to honor a state hero. Haman, who had just been invited to dine alone for a second time with the king and his wife, imagined that he must be the one to be honored, and suggested having the fortunate man escorted through the streets on the king's own horse and wearing the king's own robes. Great idea, the king responded. "Go at once. . . . Get the robe and the horse and do just as you have suggested for Mordecai the Jew, who sits at the king's gate. Do not neglect anything you have recommended" (Esther 6:10).

The whole community, of course, knew of his rivalry with Mordecai, and Haman was utterly humiliated. Before he had a chance to recover, however, the king's aides arrived and hurried him away to the banquet with Esther, where, at the climax of the evening, she identified her national origin and revealed Haman's plot against her people. The king, in a great rage, had Haman taken away to be executed on his own gallows, and then he installed Mordecai himself in the position of adviser just vacated by Haman. He then issued an edict superseding the previous one by giving the Jews the right to defend themselves (Esther 8:11–13).

The story is rich with irony, apprehension, and surprise. We don't know how it is going to come out until the very end, when our protagonists finally prevail against heroic odds. But although they did their best to act with wisdom and courage, we are quite aware that their success is due to factors beyond their control, circumstances and turns of events that appear quite arbitrary and unpredictable. Nevertheless, we are not left with the impression that they are simply lucky to have escaped by the skin of their teeth. Rather we have a tenacious conviction that every detail of this remarkable episode was unfolding according to some predetermined plan. Each person acted on his own will, doing precisely what he chose to do, yet this plan was unfolding all the time. This truth that we sense here is, perhaps, surprising because there is not a single mention of God, or even a sovereign providence, in the entire book of Esther.

In the familiar story of Job we are allowed a look behind the scenes to see God at work. Here in Esther, however, the circumstances of everyday life with all its apparent randomness and coincidence are all we see. Some things "just happen," like Esther's winning of the beauty contest, Mordecai's overhearing the plot against the king, or Xerxes' sleepless night and the secretary's reading to him the portion of the chronicles that referred to Mordecai. Haman's timing in his arrival at the court also seems coincidental. Other things are the direct result of the willful actions of individuals choosing their own course freely—Vashti's refusal to honor her husband's wishes, Haman's obsessive desire for revenge, and Mordecai's urging of Esther to petition the king. There is no "master manipulator" behind the scenes, bouncing puppets on the end of a string, yet everything works out precisely in favor of God's chosen people.

GOD DIRECTS EVEN THE DETAILS

If it is not obvious enough in the series of fortunate events that happened, stop and think for a moment about the "what if's." What if Vashti were still the queen and the Jews had no advocate in the court? What if Mordecai had been busy with something else and never heard about the assassination plot? What if the king had slept soundly the night before Haman's petition? What if Esther had not had the courage to risk her own life in petitioning the king? It is only when all these details come together that the deed is accomplished.

But this is precisely what we are being told in Romans 8:28, namely that "in all things God works for the good of those who love him, who have been called according to his purpose." It isn't that things "just happen." It isn't fate or karma. It is the intentional governance of a sovereign God who is capable of directing the smallest detail of His creation toward the accomplishment of His purpose. Remember what we said earlier as we examined the idea of sovereignty? We suggested that God is, after all, the author of the whole of history. The one writing the story is certainly capable of arranging the details to be sure his characters arrive at their proper goal or destiny.

So we are confident that every detail of our lives is under God's control. And what does Romans 8:28 say He is doing with all those details? It says He is working for the good of those who love Him. Actually the Greek word used in Romans 8:28 is the word *sunergeo*. It is richer than the simple word for work. The word for work would be *ergon,* from which we get words like "ergonomics," an applied science concerned with efficiency and safety. The word used here includes that idea, but adds the prefix *sun,* which means "with." The whole word, *sunergeo,* means "working together," and it raises up the whole idea of cooperation, each part contributing to the whole. In fact, the word was sometimes used to describe the craft of weaving. What the Bible says, then, is that God is "weaving together" every aspect and detail of our lives in the accomplishment of His great plan and purpose for us.

The word evokes for us the image of a great tapestry, precisely woven to create a picture of beauty and complexity. The art of tapestry involves an exquisite interweaving of literally thousands of individual threads in a complex and precise pattern from which emerges an often elaborate picture. You have heard of the "warp and woof" of our daily lives. The reference is to this art of weaving. The "warp" are the long, vertical threads, and the "woof" are the brightly colored horizontal threads that must be carefully woven into the warp and tightly overlapped so that the vertical threads disappear. Only the horizontal threads are visible, in such a precise combination that they form the final picture. Throughout the history of the art, tapestries have often depicted detailed scenes from the Bible or other historic events. What a wonderful image to describe the way in which God uses thousands of events and happenings in our lives, things seemingly unrelated, weaving them together in an intricate pattern to create the whole lovely, and perhaps unexpected, picture of our lives!

In the story of Esther, Haman lived by the typical Persian view of "chance fate" in which everyone used his own wit and wisdom to wend his way through a network of blind chance in an effort to accomplish his own will in the long run. We know many who live in the same way today. Some might become pessimistic in such an unpredictable world, but the more capable ones, like Haman, are quite confident they can engineer events to bring about their own desires.

Mordecai, in contrast, believed very much in human initiative, but he recognized that these human efforts would have to be used by a greater power. "If you remain silent at this time," he warned Esther, "relief and deliverance for the Jews will arise from another place, but you and your father's family will perish. And who knows but that you have come to royal position for such a time as this?" (Esther 4:14).

The final outcome, in which Haman is hanged on his own gallows ("hoist with his own petard" as Shakespeare might describe it) and Mordecai is given his position of power, ultimately confirms Mordecai's confidence in a God who works all things together "for the good of those who love him, who have been called according to his purpose."

DETAILS WOVEN TOGETHER FOR GOOD

So God's Word gives us this wonderful and encouraging picture of the way in which God weaves together all the events of our lives in the creation of a masterpiece of beauty and perfection. Every individual thread, no matter how apparently insignificant, no matter how colorful or plain, has its place in the larger picture. What also emerges from this description is the realization that most of the threads of our lives, viewed in isolation, will make very little sense, and may seem quite insignificant in and of themselves. But woven together, they take on a meaning far beyond anything we could have anticipated.

It is entirely possible that some of the most difficult or disappointing or even detestable experiences of our lives may be just the threads that, by their color and contrast, bring out the most exquisite beauty in the final picture. Perhaps an experience of humiliating failure or severe loss, so painful that we find it thoroughly devastating, will be used by God to shape the very heart of His masterpiece.

Visitors to Florence, Italy, make it a point to see Michelangelo's unsurpassed masterpiece of sculpture, *David,* and are regularly struck with awe and wonder. But their appreciation grows when they learn that other sculptors turned down the piece of marble from which it was carved because of its flaws. Michelangelo worked with those flaws to create something superbly beautiful. And that is precisely what God is committed to do with the flaws in our lives—*if* we will work with Him.

One of the fascinating things about a tapestry is that instead of working from the front, as rug weavers do, and watching the pattern emerge, tapestry makers work from the back, following a rather nonsensical pattern actually called a *cartoon.* From this side, one cannot see the beautiful picture that is emerging on the other side. Likewise it is generally true that we cannot see the pattern of our lives as God sees it. As a result, what often looks like a ridiculous cartoon to us is actually shaping up as a design of beauty and genius beyond our imagination from

God's perspective. We cannot see how the disappointments and struggles and failures or even the mundane events of daily living can add up to anything great. But God promises that He is at work in all of them. On His own honor He promises that He is weaving them into a tapestry of absolute delight for His loved ones.

J. R. R. Tolkien, in his poetic account of creation in the book *The Silmarillion,* used a different, but equally powerful, image. He described a symphony in which the creator or composer, Iluvatar, had established the themes and then invited his creation to join in the song. As each made his contribution, Iluvatar wove all the harmonies together to enhance the music. When a rebel by the name of Melkor purposefully introduced chaos and discord into the symphony, the resulting dissonance was terrible and frightening. But then Iluvatar wove an even more complex theme that embraced the dissonance, lifting the music to a higher and more thrilling and dramatic expression than before. "No theme may be played that hath not its uttermost source in me," the creator and composer explained, "nor can any alter the music in my despite. For he that attempteth this shall prove but mine instrument in the devising of things more wonderful, which he himself hath not imagined."

A wonderful insight that emerges from this study is the fact that the key word in Romans 8:28, *sunergeo,* is the foundation of our word "synergism." Synergism describes the interaction of various agents or conditions in such a way that the total effect is greater than the sum of the individual effects. And of course this is just the right word to describe what God is promising here. When two or more people work together and the mutual interaction stimulates each to a higher plane than they might have achieved on their own, we call that synergism. Something is happening here that takes us beyond our individual limitations and creates something new and dynamic and beautiful.

And this is what God is promising in our lives. Our own efforts inevitably fall short or fail. Whatever we try to create on our own could never amount to more than, as Isaiah describes it, "filthy rags," destined for destruction. But with the sovereign God of the universe who loves us and has an inconceivable destiny in mind for us, everything we are and everything we do is woven together into this magnificent tapestry, blended together in this extraordinary symphony, which will delight the hearts of all who are privileged to be involved in it. What an incredible God we have been called to love and to serve!

Chapter Six

AND IT WAS

VERY GOOD

Romans 8:22–30

The lights had gone out suddenly, and, in the darkness, thunder rumbled ominously as the storm rolled toward us. Just before sunset, from beneath the heavy cumulonimbus clouds hovering over the naked prairie, several narrow funnels had snaked toward the horizon, flicking back and forth like the tail of a cat waiting to pounce on its unsuspecting prey. Now, blind to the storm's approach, we could only wait and pray in the anxious darkness.

Few experiences are as terrifying as the approach of some potential evil or disaster when we simply can't see how it's going to turn out. Perhaps your child has been severely injured in an accident and clings to life by a thread. How is it going to end? Your reputation, and with it your security, is threatened by some humiliating failure. The person you have loved with all your heart has just abandoned you, and what you can see of the road ahead is grim and desolate.

Yet the future, which to us is obscured in darkness and beyond our control, is quite clear to God. He assures us He has it well in hand. Indeed, He has made us a simply enormous promise: No matter how things might look to us, no matter how threatening our circumstances may appear, in His sovereignty He is working all things together for the good of those who love Him.

It is important to remember that God nowhere promises that nothing bad will ever happen to us. It is tempting to interpret Psalm 91 to say that God will allow no evil ever to touch us, no disaster ever to come near us—so tempting in fact that this is the very passage Satan used to tempt Jesus, but Jesus would have none of it. He knew the cross was on the horizon for Him, but He also knew that something good—no, not just "something good," but the greatest possible good—would come of that suffering. And He knew that was the promise—the *only* promise—His Father would make to Him in a fallen and broken world. In all things, good or bad in our experience, God is working toward an ultimate good.

DEFINING GOOD

But what does He mean by "good"? Do we really understand "good" at all? How would we define it? It's good because . . . well, why? Because it gives us pleasure? Because it sustains our lives? Because it preserves life on a universal scale? Is life particularly worth preserving? On what basis will we determine what we really mean by goodness?

Throughout history thoughtful men and women have tried to define this fundamental concept and found it to be more difficult than they anticipated. Some have concluded that a thing is "good" if it brings the greatest benefit to the greatest number of people. But although this sounds good, on closer examination it's really not very helpful. For one thing, it's redundant. "Benefit" means "good." So all we have said is that a thing is "good" if it brings good, but we still don't know what good is. Besides, is a thing really good if it only benefits the majority? What if, like slavery in our own history, it comes at great cost to the minority? Is that good?

So what is good? Is a thing good if it brings the least pain? Is it good because the majority believe it is good? Is it good because the human race has historically agreed about it? Maybe we must simply make up our own definition and say a thing is good because our culture has defined it as good, and other cultures can define as good whatever they want. If that is the case, then good must always be changing. Abortion, for example, used to be bad, no matter what the circumstances, for that was the consensus. But in 1973 apparently we changed our minds. Is current law really the only standard we have to judge what is good and what is bad? Is there no greater standard by which to judge the law itself?

Perhaps something is good because it is selfless. That sounds noble. But then again, maybe a thing is really good only if it serves the self. Or maybe it's good because it "works." Or maybe just because it "feels" good. There have been defenders for all these definitions, but they all fall short on close examination. None seems adequate to define this basic concept of goodness. For the central role that the idea of "the good" plays in our lives, it is surprising that we are so far from defining it.

Or maybe it's not so surprising. If the Good, in an

ultimate sense, judges *us* and our conduct, then perhaps we will want to dispute the judgment. Perhaps we will find that no definition of the good except our own will be acceptable to us. Yes, if we are honest, that's what we want—or think we want. To be the final arbiter of what conduct is acceptable. "I want to do what's good for *me.*" Have you heard that before? Ah, yes, we will be our own gods, *knowing good and evil!* Have you heard *that* before?

The oldest warning to the human race is that along that path lies certain death. And the reason is that "good" is not something we are asked to *define.* "Good" is something we must simply *recognize.* If goodness exists at all, it exists apart from us. We may cooperate with it, or we may defy it, each choice having particular and indelible consequences, but goodness itself is indifferent to us. It will not change its face to please us. It will remain precisely what it is, whether we acknowledge it or not.

Where, then, might we encounter goodness? And how will we recognize it? Three of the gospel writers vividly recall an encounter that Jesus had with a young man who ran up to Him, calling Him a "good" teacher and asking Him about the "good" that might be required of him. Jesus, as He often did, surprised the listeners with His answer. He said, "Why do you call me good? No one is good—except God alone."

THE SUPREME GOOD

In the Bible, the supreme good is never a matter of speculation. God Himself is "the Good." He is the source of goodness, He is the measure of goodness, He is the personification of goodness. His very character is the definition of "the Good." There is nothing arbitrary or debatable about the Good. Good is what God is. Good is what God does. There is no good apart from Him. Jesus Himself is not good apart from God. One cannot know the Good unless he knows God, and he cannot experience the Good unless he is in a right relationship with God and doing what God wills, because what God wills is good—always good. Jesus confessed that the only reason for His goodness was that He always did the will of the Father.

God's revelation of Himself in history was a revelation of His goodness. Do you remember when Moses on Mount Sinai asked to see God? All of us wonder, *What would it be like to see God?* God replied, "I will cause all my *goodness* to pass in front of you" (italics added). You see, goodness is fundamental to who God is, to His character. "I will cause all my goodness to pass in front of you, and I will proclaim my name, the Lord" (Exodus 33:19). And that is exactly what He did. In Exodus 34 we read,

> And the Lord descended in the cloud, and stood with him there, and proclaimed the name of the Lord. And the Lord passed by before him [now we get to see God's goodness!], and proclaimed, The Lord, The Lord God, merciful and gracious, longsuffering, and abundant in goodness and truth, keeping mercy for thousands, forgiving iniquity and transgression and sin, and that will by no means clear the guilty [He would not be a good God if he did not recognize what is bad]." (vv. 5–7 KJV)

All these things, then, constitute God's goodness: justice no less than mercy, grace as well as truth, forbearance that does not compromise holiness, and, fundamental to the whole list, His own initiative in preparing a way by which we might ultimately share His fellowship and delight. And if this picture is not enough, the term "abundant in goodness" stresses His incomparable *generosity* in sharing all this with us. J. I. Packer, in *Knowing God,* says that generosity is "the focal point of God's moral perfection. . . . Generosity means a disposition to give to others in a way which has no mercenary motive and is not limited by what the recipients deserve, but consistently goes beyond it." What a wonderful definition! "Generosity expresses the simple wish that others should have what they need to make them happy."[1] God is abundant in goodness; He is committed to give us what we need to make us happy.

In this light Psalm 145:9, 14–16 says, "The Lord is good to all; he has compassion on all he has made. . . . The Lord upholds all those who fall and lifts up all who are bowed down. The eyes of all look to you, and you give them their food at the proper time. You open your hand and satisfy the desires of every living thing." That's what God does— far beyond what we deserve. God in His goodness encourages us, He heals us, He seeks daily to satisfy the desires of our hearts. He delights in meeting our needs: physical and emotional, intellectual and aesthetic. He gives us our meals to savor; He gives us beautiful things to admire, adventures to experience; He gives us quiet moments to read and reflect, particular possessions to treasure; He gives us such simple refreshment as a night of rest. He knows our needs and He gives abundantly. Psalms 106 and 107 voice our "thanks to the Lord, for he is good," and go on to catalog all the times of deliverance and provision that God makes for His people.

WHAT GOD'S GOODNESS MEANS TO US

In this light, the Bible is rich with expressions of what God's goodness means to us. Deuteronomy 30:9 says that, when His people are obedient, "The Lord your God will make you most prosperous in all the work of your hands and in the fruit of your womb, the young of your livestock and the crops of your land. The Lord will again delight in you." The idea of prosperity and delight is at the heart of the biblical word for "good." The KJV says He will "rejoice over thee *for good*" (italics added). Therefore when God says, "I'll work all things together for good," He's talking about prosperity, He's talking about delight, He's talking about the most favorable circumstances for you. The word may be applied to scenic beauty or to things going well. It is used to describe the "*good* and spacious land, a land flowing with milk and honey" (Exodus 3:8, italics added) that He promised His people, which meant not only what it presently possessed but its future potential, in terms of fruitfulness and "pleasantness." The Bible expresses God's concern for our good in a beautiful picture of a person sitting under his own vine and enjoying creation.

Whenever the word is applied to one's heart, it means well-being, joy and happiness in your heart. In 1 Kings 8:66 we read of God's people going to their tents "joyful and glad in heart for all the good things the Lord had done for his servant David," suggesting the idea of being fulfilled and satisfied, in a frame of heart to celebrate. All these are hints of what He has in mind when He promises to work in all circumstances "for the good of those who love him."

But the expression of goodness that perhaps carries the most profound implications is in that wonderful and familiar story of creation from Genesis 1. This is the first expression of goodness in the Bible. In Genesis 1:4 God had just called light into being. Can you imagine it? Out of nothing! And, He said, that's "good." Then when water had condensed out of the atmosphere and found its place, clinging to our planet, making life possible, God again looked at it and said, "This also is good." And when vegetation in all its variegated splendor covered the earth, God yet again proclaimed this goodness. The differentiation of sun, moon, and stars marking seasons, days, and years received the same evaluation. When you and I look in awe upon the heavens and express our grand delight, we are joining God in an analysis of His creation. And it is the same with His animal creatures.

When God used the word "good" (the Hebrew word *tobh*) to describe His creation, He was telling us that all the things He had made were not just pleasant and beautiful, but they were actually good and perfect, in every sense adequate for the purpose He had designed. He was not trying out experiments to see what might work. He had fit it all together precisely as it ought to be for the maximum benefit and beauty. In support of this interpretation is the fact that on two occasions when His work was only partially complete, He refrained from declaring it to be good. The second day He didn't say anything was good, and the reason was apparently that what happened the second day wasn't complete. An atmosphere was forming, but not until it was complete and the water necessary to support life was in place on the third day did He finally say it was good.

And to make the case more strongly, in the account of the final day of creation in the second chapter, God even stated explicitly that one aspect of His creation was "not good" (v. 18). It was not good that the man should be alone. In other words, humanity without the sexual differentiation of male and female was not good. The creation of human persons in His image is complete and good only when we have both men and women and when each person gives his or her best to a community or offers his or her uniqueness to the other in marriage, instead of just living for themselves. Indeed, the account of creation in Genesis 2 climaxes with the male and the female giving themselves wholly to each other. Our culture cannot succeed in blurring God's purposeful distinction between male and female without doing itself great injury, because in God's economy, a thing is "good" only when it is perfectly suited to its purpose. God made all things the way they ought to be and He called them "good." He wants, when they are broken, to make them good again. And that is what He wants for each of us.

When God says, therefore, that He is working all things together "for good," He is saying something magnificent! He is saying that He is forming them so that they will fit together perfectly as working parts of a whole and comprehensive "paradise" like that of Eden. He is saying He is preparing us, His children, for a day when all things will be what they ought to be, when prosperity and peace and delight will not be things we only glimpse or dream of—they will be the order of the day. God's blessings will rain down on us like a summer shower in Eden!

GOOD AND EVIL IN OUR LIVES

That is His promise, but we must explore one more aspect of it that is very significant. We would all love to share the "goodness" of Eden. But what is to keep the new Eden God has promised from falling into the same brokenness as the first? We may not doubt that God can make a perfect paradise *without* creatures capable of choosing evil. But how can God put sinful people like us into Paradise without destroying it? In this light it is important to know that God did not create evil, but it was absolutely necessary that He allow it. And though this is a controversy that has gone on for millennia, let me see if I can support that conclusion.

Evil, we must understand, is no *thing*. It was not, indeed it could not have been, created, for it has no substance. Only good things were created. In fact, there is no such thing as "badness" in the same way that there is "goodness." Evil is only the twisting of the good. It is an exercise of the will to take something good and pervert or distort it. In a letter to his good friend Arthur Greeves, C. S. Lewis gives this insight: "There can be good without evil, but no evil without good. . . . Evil is a parasite. It is there only because good is there for it to spoil and confuse."

But of course, although evil does not exist as an entity in itself, evil *people* do. And evil people are not people who were created evil, but people who were created with a free will, and who have chosen to exercise that will to distort what is good. You might ask why God made people who were capable of badness. Why didn't He make us capable only of goodness? But you see, we only reflect the image of God if we, like Him, exercise our will in making choices. The rest of creation simply reacts as it is conditioned to react. If we are to experience and appreciate the good as God appreciates it, we must choose the good from our own will. In that sense, goodness is like love. Love is simply not love if it does not involve a choice. God made people who were capable of making choices. And He did this because He wanted us to have the opportunity to know and experience what is good. So for us to be capable of experiencing goodness, God had to make us capable of badness—that is, capable of choices.

The problem is, we don't have God's essentially good character. That is God's character alone. God gives us the ability to make choices, but having no innate goodness, we ultimately prove incapable of making good choices on our own. So how are we ever going to get beyond our failure? How can Paradise ever be restored? God is promising a new Eden here. Yet it seems impossible to have a place where everything turns out good if that place allows *us* to muddle about in it.

The answer is that we were never asked to exercise goodness on our own. That would be an impossible task. When you struggle to be good, it's more than a struggle; it's impossible. It's like asking you to pour water out of a jar that contains only oil. You can't do it. It's not there. Goodness, as Jesus said, is in God alone. *All we were ever asked to do was to take our lives and offer them back to the Lord so His goodness could flow through us.* We are not asked to do what we are incapable of doing; we are asked to surrender. And when we do, God begins to remake us from the heart.

Christ, of course, has atoned for our sins. But we may worry that our free will would leave us vulnerable to sin once again, even in a world that has been redeemed. After all, Adam and Eve still sinned in a perfect world! But you understand, our capacity for sin cannot contaminate heaven as it did earth, for in heaven all things are made new. We might compare it to baking cookies. Cookies contain some "nasty" tasting things, like shortening and baking soda and raw eggs, ingredients that, if consumed by themselves, would likely make you sick. But the final product embraces those things and transforms them, changing their fundamental character so the end result is something truly delicious. If you are a cook you know you can include bitter herbs, sour cream, or perhaps a wretched fungus like yeast and still come up with something good. How does that happen? The bad things are incorporated together to make something good. That's what God does with us. That is why we, even though we are capable of sin, can be incorporated into heaven, for His goodness transforms us. But it is our choice whether to surrender ourselves to Him to be made new.

For me, there is symbolic significance in the way God describes the days of creation in Genesis 1. Surprisingly, He does *not* say, "the morning and the evening were the first day." Rather He says, "And there was evening, and there was morning—the first day." God in His ultimate goodness is always moving from darkness to light; He's always moving from chaos to order; He's always moving from despair to hope, from defeat to victory, from death to life. Therefore every day in His presence is a dawning; it is an awakening, not an ending. It is the opening up of a myriad of new possibilities. Hell, of course, is the opposite. It is the closing off of all our opportunities as darkness falls over all those things that might have been. But heaven, to which He invites every one of us, is a new dawn every day.

That is the good He is offering every believer in Romans 8:28. If we will surrender to Him, He will wrap His arms around us in spite of all the distortions of His goodness that we have perpetrated; embracing all the suffering and pain of our broken world; and transforming them into something more beautiful and more joyful and more complete than we could ever have imagined. Indeed, when that final day, that ultimate Sabbath rest, approaches, God will be able to look at the Paradise He has established for all who will accept it, and see all that He has done, and declare that this, finally, is (as He said on the last day of creation) *very good,* exceedingly good. At that moment the world's last night will have ended, and, as that spiritual says, "that great, gettin'-up mornin'" will have begun! It is the ultimate dawn for which believing hearts have longed throughout the dark and troubling night. As the first rays of the rising sun strike our faces, we who have trusted in Christ will leap from our beds to exult in a world made new—new to the very heart—our hearts! That's a day you won't mind getting out of bed. The world is made new and so are you.

NOTE

1. J. I. Packer, *Knowing God* (Downers Grove, Ill.: InterVarsity, 1973), 146.

Chapter Seven

LOVING

GOD

Mark 12:28–34

𝒯t is an absolutely astonishing promise, when you stop to think about it, perhaps the most far-reaching and encouraging promise that could ever be made to us under any circumstances. That God—the sovereign God who controls every detail of the universe and of history —would make us a promise, on His honor, to take every circumstance, every detail of our lives and weave them together to accomplish something totally and unequivocally good for us, is, I think, a promise so vast and so breathtaking that likely not one of us has really grasped it.

And yet that is what He has done! This promise dwarfs any suffering or discouragement and reduces to the point of irrelevance any bad thing that might trouble us.

But there is one absolutely crucial part of this promise that we have not yet explored. And that is the question of who may honestly claim this promise. Is it directed to all of us indiscriminately? Is God promising to take every bad thing that has ever happened to anyone and make it turn out good for that person in the long run? I am afraid that this wishful conclusion cannot be sustained. The promise is indeed remarkable, but it is directed exclusively to those who love God. "And we know that in all things God works for the good *of those who love him*" (Romans 8:28, italics added). And here, of course, is the "catch." We would all dearly love to claim this promise, but a question for us is implicit within it: Do we really love God? In all honesty, is God—His purpose, His welfare, and His reputation—the true and exclusive object of your desire? That, I am afraid, is what it means truly to love someone!

In an interview with the *Washington Post,* a prominent movie star and "spokesperson" for popular culture had this to say:

> The most pleasurable journey you take is through yourself....The only sustaining love involvement is with yourself....When you look back on your life and try to figure out where you've been and where you're going, when you look at your work, your love affairs, your marriages, your children, your pain, your happiness—when you examine all that closely, what you really find out is that the only person you really go to bed with is yourself....The only thing you have is working to the consummation of your own identity. And that's what I've been trying to do all my life. (Shirley MacLaine)[1]

I don't think she's alone in that commitment. We have spent most of the last several decades, if not much longer, trying desperately to love ourselves. We are obsessed with our own health and our own wealth and our own reputations. Our school children chant endless mantras of self-esteem. We will go to any seminar that promises us success and happiness or self-fulfillment. And yet for all our affluence, for all our self-absorption, we are more miserable and more empty than ever, filled only with anxiety and self-doubt.

And the reason for our lack of contentment and joy is that we have not really learned to love God. C. S. Lewis persuades us in *Surprised by Joy* that the fundamental desire of our hearts, whether we know it or not, is for God, and therefore in seeking the fulfillment of that desire anywhere else, we are guaranteed disappointment. It's like trying to assuage your thirst with a bagel; it won't work. We are made to love God—first, last, and above all else—and should we refuse, we are condemned to an eternal unhappiness and discontent.

By contrast, Psalm 37:4 says, "Delight yourself in the Lord and he will give you the desires of your heart." That's a beautiful verse. Do you believe that promise? It is our invitation to love God and find our joy in Him forever.

THE MOST IMPORTANT DUTY

In Mark 12:28, an expert in the Law, recognizing Jesus' remarkable wisdom and insight, came to Him and asked a question that a thoughtful teacher of the Law might have considered for a long time. He said, "Of all the commandments, which is the most important?" What, in other words, is the most important duty of a man or a woman? And Jesus answered by quoting from the sixth chapter of Deuteronomy:

> "The most important one," answered Jesus, "is this: 'Hear, O Israel, the Lord our God, the Lord is one. Love the Lord

your God with all your heart and with all your soul and with all your mind and with all your strength.'The second is this:'Love your neighbor as yourself.'There is no commandment greater than these." (vv. 29–31)

Love the Lord your God with all your heart and with all your soul and with all your mind and with all your strength. That's the challenge. The placement of that command at the introduction to the Old Testament covenant with Israel as they prepared to enter the Promised Land, and its identification as the greatest commandment by Jesus at the climax of His earthly teaching, establish it as the very heart of God's revelation to us. Do you want to know what is most important? Here it is: Love the Lord your God. You and I must recognize this. Nothing in our lives is more important than learning to love God, and nothing else in our lives will really fit together until we do.

But our experience tells us this is very difficult to do. No doubt this is the result of our sin, but the fact is, we *don't* love the Lord with all our heart, soul, mind, and strength. Even those who have given themselves to a lifetime of service to the Lord often fail to understand this challenge. Kathryn Spink, in a book called *The Miracle of Love,* told about a monk who went to Mother Teresa complaining that his order's rules were interfering with his ministry. "My vocation is to work for lepers," he told her. "I want to spend myself for lepers." But Mother Teresa looked at him awhile and then she smiled and said, "Brother, your vocation is not to work for lepers; your vocation is to belong to Jesus." Above everything else, loving God means giving ourselves to Him—not to an occupation, not to an idea, not to a goal, but to Him.

LOVING GOD FOR HIMSELF

Here then is the question—a very difficult question —that all of us need to ask ourselves: Do we truly love God? Do we love God for who He is, or do we only appreciate Him for what He can give us? There is a profound difference! Alexander the Great of Macedonia had two friends, Hephestion and Craterus, of whom he said, "Hephestion loves me because I am Alexander; Craterus loves me because I am King Alexander." Which one truly loved Alexander? Which one loved Alexander's heart? There is a great difference between loving someone for who the person is, and loving someone for what that person can give you. To love someone only for what he can give you is really only to love yourself.

"True love," Thomas Watson wrote in 1663 in a book called *All Things for Good,* "is not mercenary. You need not hire a mother to love her child: a soul deeply in love with God needs not to be hired by rewards. It cannot but love Him for that luster of beauty that sparkles forth in Him." Why should we love God? We should love Him for who He is. We should love Him because He is infinitely wise. We should love Him because He is awesomely beautiful as reflected in His works of creation and His acts of grace. We should love Him because He is the very essence of goodness. We should love Him because He is boundless and free. We should love Him because He is utterly reliable and full of truth. We should love Him because He is "slow to anger and abounding in love and faithfulness" (Exodus 34:6). We should love Him because He is breathtakingly holy and uncompromisingly just. We should love Him because He is powerful beyond imagination and yet gentle beyond hope. You see, if we stop to think about it, What's not to love? How could we possibly know Him and not love Him?

Yet we do not love Him, not without a divided heart. In our silly attempts to escape the claim of His love upon our lives, we begin to love the things of this world more than we love Him. But think about this. What does the world really give us for all the love we offer it? The world does not satisfy. It gives us some pleasure, to be sure, just enough to make us ask for more, just enough to lead us another step in our pursuit of happiness, but it does not satisfy. And should it keep us distracted in that pursuit all the way to the grave, what then has it really given us? But of God, David says in Psalm 17:14–15, "You still the hunger of those you cherish; . . . And I—in righteousness I will see your face; when I awake, I will be satisfied with seeing your likeness." An old spiritual gives expression to this love from the heart:

> In the morning when I rise, Give me Jesus. Just about the break of day, Give me Jesus. Oh, when I come to die, Give me Jesus. You may have all this world, Give me Jesus.

That's the expression of a heart that has come to know who God is and has begun to seek to love Him.

The things of this world, which we love so much and in which we invest so much, cannot remove trouble from your mind. But God can give you peace when nothing else can. He can "turn the shadow of death into morning," as His Word says (Amos 5:8 NKJV). The things of this world only take your love; they do not return it. Jesus said, "If anyone loves me, . . . My Father will love him, and we will come to him and make our home with him" (John 14:23). The things of this world have a very brief life, and eventually they decay and die. "But God," Psalm 73:26 says, "is the strength of my heart and my portion forever." The things of the world will very likely keep you out of heaven, as Jesus noted in regard to the possessions of the rich, but His goal is to prepare a place for us in heaven, and then to come and take us to be with Him that we can enjoy it as He does.

REASONS FOR LOVING GOD

Do you need reasons to love the Lord? "I love the Lord," the psalmist says in Psalm 116:1–6, 12,

> for he heard my voice; he heard my cry for mercy. Because he turned his ear to me, I will call on him as long as I live. The cords of death entangled me, the anguish of the grave came upon me; I was overcome by trouble and sorrow. Then I called on the name of the Lord: "O Lord, save me!" The Lord is gracious and righteous; our God is full of compassion. The Lord protects the simplehearted; when I was in great need, he saved me. . . . How can I repay the Lord for all his goodness to me?

There is a man who had learned there were good reasons for loving God.

"We love [God]," John wrote in his first New Testament letter, "because he first loved us" (4:19). J. I. Packer, in his book *Knowing God,* pointed out that God's love for us is His unlimited generosity, directed to us not as a whole, but individually and personally, and despite the fact that we in no way deserve it. It's a love that drove Him to come in person and give up His lifeblood for us on the cross. If you get even a glimpse of that, doesn't it begin to stir your soul? Psalm 73:25 expresses beautifully the response of the heart that finally grasps this: "Whom have I in heaven but you? And earth has nothing I desire besides you."

We have abundant reasons for loving God. And although we may love Him simply for who He is, nevertheless He has made numerous and generous promises to those who love Him. First Corinthians 2:9 (NKJV) says, "Eye has not seen, nor ear heard, nor have entered into the heart of man the things which God has prepared for those who love Him." There are, Paul is assuring us, unimaginable rewards—more than you can even fathom, more than you can think of in your wildest imagination —prepared "for those who love him."

But wait a minute, you may be saying, didn't we just say that we should love God for who He is, rather than for what He gives us? Yes, but the distinction between the two is so fine as to be almost invisible. It is the distinction that, can it be made, enables Job to say, "Though he slay me, yet will I trust him" (Job 13:15)—that's love, for the rewards, you see, may not be immediate, or even fathomable, and Job recognized that. Those who truly love God for who He is, those who have really matured in their love, may understand the astonishing testimony of Habakkuk in the Old Testament, who concluded after a challenging encounter with God, "Though the fig tree does not bud and there are no grapes on the vines, though the olive crop fails and the fields produce no food, though there are no sheep in the pen and no cattle in the stalls, yet I will rejoice in the Lord, I will be joyful in God my Savior" (Habakkuk 3:17). That may be the advanced course in loving God. When we experience a loss, we're not sure we can simply rejoice in God, but that's our goal, moving to that place where we find such joy in Him that we recognize all else is second to that love. God is worthy of our love whether He gives us rewards or not.

But one of the beautiful and remarkable things about God is that although this is true, nevertheless He is almost shameless about offering us rewards. My most often quoted mentor, C. S. Lewis, in his grand sermon "The Weight of Glory" expressed this most memorably:

> If there lurks in most modern minds the notion that to desire our own good and earnestly to hope for the enjoyment of it is a bad thing, I submit that this notion has crept in from Kant and the Stoics and is no part of Christian faith. Indeed, if we consider the unblushing promises of reward and the staggering nature of the rewards promised in the Gospels, it would seem that Our Lord finds our desires not too strong but too weak.

Then comes this great line from Lewis:

> We are half-hearted creatures, fooling about with drink and sex and ambition when infinite joy is offered us, like an ignorant child who wants to go on making mud pies in a slum because he cannot imagine what is meant by an offer of a holiday at the sea. We are far too easily pleased.

We try to find our joy in empty worldly pleasures when God has offered us true joy. And then this,

> We must not be troubled by unbelievers when they say that this promise of reward makes the Christian life a mercenary affair. There are different kinds of rewards.

> There is the reward which has no natural connection with the things you do to earn it and is quite foreign to the desires that ought to accompany those things. Money is not the natural reward of love; that is why we call a man mercenary if he marries a woman for the sake of her money. But marriage is the proper reward for a real lover, and he is not mercenary for desiring it. . . . The proper rewards are not simply tacked on to the activity for which they are given, but are the activity itself in consummation.[2]

Rewards simply describe what it is that we get when we receive God. To receive God is to obtain His care and His protection. "I love you, O Lord, my strength," David said in Psalm 18:1. "The Lord is my rock, my fortress and my deliverer; my God is my rock, in whom I take refuge. He is my shield and the horn of my salvation, my stronghold. I call to the Lord, who is worthy of praise, and I am saved from my enemies" (vv. 2–3). You see, it is a reward, but it is a reward intrinsic to the character of God. To be in Him is to be protected from all ills. "He who dwells in the shelter of the Most High will rest in the shadow of the Almighty," Psalm 91:1 says. "'Because he loves me,' says the Lord, 'I will rescue him; I will protect him, for he acknowledges my name. He will call upon me, and I will answer him; I will be with him in trouble, I will deliver him and honor him. With long life will I satisfy him and show him my salvation'" (vv. 14–16). All those things are rewards, but they are rewards intrinsic to the character of God.

KNOWING GOD IN ORDER TO LOVE HIM

All these incredible benefits are simply a description of what life is like in God's embrace. Isaiah says, "[Those] who bind themselves to the Lord to serve him, to love the name of the Lord, and to worship him, all who keep the Sabbath without desecrating it and who hold fast to my covenant—these I will bring to my holy mountain and give them joy in my house" (Isaiah 56:6–7). It was desire for this joy that drove C. S. Lewis's lifelong search. He, like most of us, thought joy was a feeling of excitement or delight that might be aroused in us by some experience, perhaps of earthly beauty or pleasure. But the feeling always receded in the pursuit. It's a sad thing to celebrate our inalienable right to pursue happiness. It's really not an adequate goal, because happiness is not an object, and therefore can never be grasped. We can chase happiness forever and we'll never grasp it, as the writer of Ecclesiastes reminds us. Joy simply describes our state of fullness and satisfaction when we have obtained the Real Object, namely God Himself, for whom our souls long. To pursue joy aside from its object would be like attempting to find satisfaction for our thirst without water. Water is the source of our thirst's satisfaction. There will be no satisfaction without it, as there is no joy without God.

This, of course, is why all things work together for good for those who love God. Having placed themselves in His embrace, they must inevitably find themselves in the place of ultimate good. And anything at all that points them in that direction, that draws them into His embrace, no matter how painful, will have been for the good. It's why Aleksandr Solzhenitsyn could say of the Soviet gulag, the most horrible experience that a person might imagine, "Bless you, Prison, for having been in my life." Why did he say such a preposterous thing? Because that experience had driven him into the arms of God! If we love Him for who He is, then every trial, every indignity, every disappointment, every failure will drive us more deeply into the heart of joy.

Well then, how can we learn to love God? What is the source of this love that we recognize in its importance but find so difficult to develop in our own lives? I think first of all we cannot love what we do not know. As we reflect upon His astonishing character and His unadulterated compassion for us, we may begin to love Him. But, of course, it is our sin that distorts our perspective and perverts our character even when we know the Truth. Knowing isn't enough. We will not likely learn to love God much without putting away our sin. As long as we are unwilling to deal straightforwardly and honestly with our sin, we are not going to learn to love God. This, however, cannot be done in our own strength. So we step back even further and begin with prayer. Paul prayed for the Thessalonians, "May the Lord direct your hearts into God's love and Christ's perseverance" (2 Thessalonians 3:5).

Again in Philippians 1:9 he wrote, "And this is my prayer: that your love may abound more and more in knowledge and depth of insight." And in Romans 5:5 he pointed out that "God has poured out his love into our hearts by the Holy Spirit, whom he has given us." You and I do not have within us the innate ability to love God. All these incredible promises that the Lord offers to those who love Him may be claimed by us only if God's Spirit is at work changing our hearts, making them capable of loving Him instead of loving only ourselves and loving ourselves so poorly that we destroy ourselves in the attempt.

MAKING THE CHOICE TO LOVE

On the practical level, then, we must pray consistently that God would make His love abound more and more in us. And then, as with all love, rather than waiting around for some magical change of heart, we must simply do what love requires, for we know what that is. "Love is patient." Will you be patient? I won't ask *can* you; I say *will* you exercise patience. "Love is kind. It does not envy, it does not boast, it is not proud. It is not rude, it is not self-seeking, it is not easily angered, it keeps no record of wrongs. Love does not delight in evil but rejoices with the truth. It always protects, always trusts, always hopes, always perseveres." You can review that definition in 1 Corinthians 13:4–7. Love, whether for God or for anyone else, never was a matter of feelings that we are called upon to generate. Love has always been a choice. Love has always been a choice to treat someone, or approach someone, in a particular way. Having done that, we find that we have truly loved. Feelings of affection and delight tend to follow those actions. We cannot depend upon feelings to precede actions.

We shall not here be able to explore all the evidence that may prove our love for God, either to Him or to ourselves. But Jesus was quite explicit with His statement, "Whoever has my commands and obeys them, he is the one who loves me" (John 14:21). So there is a test. Do we love God? It's not a matter of what feelings or emotions are stirring in our hearts. "Whoever has my commands and obeys them, he is the one who loves me." This, of course, will be true whether we can see the immediate benefit of obedience or not. To love God means ultimately to trust Him to be true to His character and to His promises. So we may simply do the right thing, regardless of how it makes us feel or what effect it seems to have at the time.

Harder, perhaps, even than obeying, and sometimes bound up with obeying, will be our willingness to suffer for our Lord. Perhaps this seems too much to ask, and God doesn't ask before we're able to give. But I must ask whether you would really believe Jesus' love for us if He had said, "Now you people have to believe that I love you. You are very dear to Me, but I am not willing to suffer for you; I'm not willing to lay down My life for you." Would you believe that He loved us? You see, there is no way to avoid it. To truly love someone is to be willing, if necessary, to suffer on that person's behalf. It doesn't mean we love suffering; we love the person and if necessary we'll suffer on his behalf.

And, of course, we will always desire to serve someone we love; we will desire to see that his reputation is protected. And finally, if we love God, we will love what He loves, and that, fundamentally, is loving one another. "If anyone says, 'I love God,' yet hates his brother," the apostle John says, "he is a liar" (1 John 4:20a). No words minced there. "For anyone who does not love his brother, whom he has seen, cannot love God, whom he has not seen. And he has given us this command: Whoever loves God must also love his brother" (vv. 20b–21).

These, then, are the fruits that must be developing in our lives if we are to claim the promise that all things will certainly work together for good for those who love God. My prayer for you, and I hope yours for me, is that grand prayer Paul offered on behalf of the Ephesians.

For this reason I kneel before the Father, from whom his whole family in heaven and on earth derives its name. I pray that out of his glorious riches he may strengthen you with power through his Spirit in your inner being, so that Christ may dwell in your hearts through faith. And I pray that you, being rooted and established in love, may have power, together with all the saints, to grasp how wide and long and high and deep is the love of Christ, and to know this love that surpasses knowledge—that you may be filled to the measure of all the fullness of God. (Ephesians 3:14–19)

And then that grand benediction:

Now to him who is able to do immeasurably more than all we ask or imagine, according to his power that is at work within us, to him be glory in the church and in Christ Jesus throughout all generations, for ever and ever! Amen. (vv. 20–21)

NOTES

1. Quoted in Charles Colson, *Loving God* (Grand Rapids: Zondervan, 1983), 11. From a *Washington Post* interview in 1977.
2. C. S. Lewis, "The Weight of Glory" in *The Weight of Glory and Other Addresses* (New York: Macmillan, 1965), 3–4.

Section Three
THE PURPOSE

Chapter Eight

ALL WE'RE

CREATED TO BE

Romans 8:28–30

Serious Christians often ask me, "How can I know God's will for my life?" (Foolishly, those who do not take faith seriously never ask.) It is an important question, the most important question a person could ask. By it people usually mean something like: "Should I get married or remain single?" "Should I go to college? And, if so, which college should I choose?" "Should I become a plumber, an engineer, a teacher, or an airline pilot?" Invariably I answer them, "I know precisely what God's will is for your life. . . . God's will is that you should become conformed to the image of Jesus Christ."

I am not being facetious when I answer this way. I mean this answer with all my heart. It is the answer that pervades Scripture, and it so far supersedes whether or not you should marry or go to college or choose to be a plumber that I can't even compare, in order of magnitude, the significance. Whatever you do, God wants you to become conformed to the image of Jesus Christ. That must be our primary concern.

You can find this answer all the way back in the first chapter of the Bible. There in that wonderful account God described the origin of all things. Light and energy burst forth into a universe previously without form and void, with nothing but darkness to cover the face of the great deep, and God said delightedly, "That's good!" At His command, vast clouds of gas and cosmic dust collapsed to form the nuclear core of our sun, space debris coalesced into rocky planets, and again God said, "This too is good." Gases, released by volcanic action and the impact of asteroids on the planet's surface and bound there by gravity, were blended by His precise hand into oceans and an atmosphere that would sustain life. And God saw that this too was good.

And then, in an awesome display of His power, He invested this inert world with life. *Bara!* the Hebrew says, created; He brought into being life itself. Vegetation spread across the crumbling surface of the planet, and land, air, and oceans were filled with teeming life. And again, God, hardly able to contain His enthusiasm, declared it to be good. It was a Paradise of unimaginable beauty and complexity. But God was not yet finished. To His Colleagues in creation, God said, Let's do something special. Let's make a being in Our own image, in Our likeness, and let them have dominion over this earth with its creatures. And that is what They did. And when He had blessed them, and encouraged them to be creative, and fruitful, and wise in their governance of this earth, He stepped back with an air of absolute satisfaction and said, "This is *very* good!" And then He stopped to admire and enjoy this magnificent accomplishment, and He gave us also the seventh day in which we might appreciate the good things that He had made and done.

It is absolutely essential that you and I understand how this all began if we are to understand what it is that God expects of us, for we are a part of this creation. He made us on purpose, and we have a special place within His world. Do you know why God made you? Human beings, formed by His hand, are a part of God's material creation. We are not gods. But we are also, according to this account, a quantum leap above everything else. Today, having abandoned God's revealed Word of truth, the rest of our world doesn't really know that. We don't know where we fit into the scheme of things. But God's Word says, Yes, you were created, but you are also in a position above the rest of creation. This is not pride or arrogance speaking, nor does it give us leave to abuse the rest of God's masterpiece. Certainly not that. It is simply our starting point for understanding everything else about ourselves. "O Lord, our Lord," Psalm 8:1, 3–9 says so eloquently,

> how majestic is your name in all the earth! . . . When I consider your heavens, the work of your fingers, the moon and the stars, which you have set in place, what is man that you are mindful of him, the son of man that you care for him? [Yet] you made him a little lower than [God] and crowned him with glory and honor. You made him ruler over the works of your hands; you put everything under his feet: all flocks and herds, and the beasts of the field, the birds of the air, and the fish of the sea, all that swim the paths of the seas. O Lord, our Lord, how majestic is your name in all the earth!

| MADE LIKE GOD

If you and I are to understand ourselves at all, and even begin to realize all the possibilities of being human, we must understand the stunning fact that not only were we created by God, but we were made like Him in remarkable ways—ways that allow us to reflect His image, and therefore to appreciate what He appreciates and to enjoy what He enjoys. There are at least five ways, evident in the early pages of Scripture, in which we may reflect the image of God. Keep in mind that the image of God is not something static that clings to us like blond hair or a tattoo. It is something dynamic; it is a potential, a capability, which may be exercised by us freely as a matter of will.

Perhaps the most obvious characteristic we share with God (having been made in His likeness), but with no other form of life, is rationality. It is quite astonishing, when you stop to think about it, that we may consider and associate abstract thoughts and ideas and communicate them to each other. Science, for all its accomplishments, has not really begun to understand this mysterious phenomenon. Periodically the scientist lays aside his work and says, "We have no idea how rationality works!" But without the ability to think and reason, we could not understand God's intentions, nor act responsibly and deliberately within His creation. So He made us in His image, sharing His rationality that we might think and act purposefully.

A second aspect of God's character that we share is the ability to enter into relationships. This is very important. Animals, of course, relate on a very basic, instinctive level—some animals live in communities, even as other animals are able to associate rudimentary stimuli in a way that resembles primitive reasoning. But no one really believes that bees are altruistic in their desire to support the hive or that mourning doves actually fall in love. Fundamental to God's character, however, is His conscious choice to love, and even to serve, first of all the other persons of the Godhead, and then us as well, His human creatures. Made like Him, we are not healthy if we seek to live only for ourselves. One of the fundamental problems with our society is that it is so totally self-referential. God says, "I made you for community. I made you to love people. I made you to serve people, and you'll not be happy or fulfilled until you do." There is a reason that the recluse who isolates himself in a cabin in the woods becomes in the end something less than human. The first man and the first woman were called upon to honor and to love each other, as well as to love their Creator, because this made them human. The ability to enter into relationships reflects God.

Third, we actually have a share in God's creativity. He, of course, creates *ex nihilo,* out of nothing. We may only work with the things He has already created. Even when a man and a woman, out of their love for each other, bring a new child to life, they have begun with the substance of their own bodies. We understand that this is God's doing. Nevertheless it is a breathtaking accomplishment, which deserves to be greeted every time with awe and wonder. Beyond that we are invited to create in a thousand other ways. We may paint pictures or compose music; we may create whole new worlds with words in story as Lewis and Tolkien and others have done so effectively; we may landscape our yards, decorate our houses, or grow gardens; we may contribute substantially to the shaping of the life and character of our children; we may invent new machines, develop new technologies, create new businesses, or lay out new cities; indeed, whole civilizations, for better or for worse, are the product of our creative ability. So we share God's creativity as well as His ability to enter into relationships and His rationality.

Fourth, it is within our power to accept the privilege and responsibility of managing and making the best of the forces and the products of nature. The Bible calls it having "dominion over" the rest of creation, and it is a very significant thing. Today many in our world challenge this, partly because it has been abused even by some who might call themselves Christian. Dominion does not mean that we exploit nature; yet the environmentalist who simply wants to leave nature to itself equally misunderstands. Dominion is really a stewardship for God's creation. It doesn't mean we squander or abuse it. It means we steward it, we tend it, we nourish it so that it lives up to its potential. It is the gardener's approach to the whole earth, weeding and feeding, protecting and nurturing, planting and tilling and harvesting with the goal of maximum productivity. We've got a lot to learn in this area of stewardship of the earth, but it's part of our calling to reflect God's image. Our lives should come to reflect God's lordship over all things and His truly exquisite care of all He has so lovingly created.

Finally and most comprehensively, we reflect God's image by acting in a way that pleases Him, acting in a way that reflects His holy character. We generally refer to this as our ability to choose and to act morally. But more to the point, perhaps, is Jesus' explanation of the motivation that guided His moral choices. He said, "I seek not to please myself but him who sent me" (John 5:30). The essence of righteousness is not to do whatever seems right in our own eyes, or what's pleasing to us, but rather that which, because it conforms to God's good character, is pleasing to Him. J. I. Packer in his book *Knowing Man* says, "The biblical idea of God's law is not, in the first instance, that of a public legal code . . . but of friendly authoritative instruction such as a wise father gives his children. . . . God's law is his kindly word to us as our Creator who cares for us and wants to lead us into rewarding paths."[1] God's rules are the way to play the game, and a kindly Creator will certainly let us know what the rules are.

GOD'S INSTRUCTIONS

Satan's earliest, most effective, and most destructive weapon of deception, first practiced in the Garden of Eden, was his suggestion that God's rules were intended to keep us from true happiness and fulfillment. What a ridiculous suggestion! Conversely, he said, this happiness and fulfillment would come to us by breaking God's laws and doing whatever seemed right and pleasing to us. Adam and Eve did it and of course learned the opposite. Don't you feel like an idiot when you fall for the same lie as our first parents? We've made Satan's job so easy. He hasn't even had to vary his temptation since the first generation of the human race.

God's laws are simply His instructions for running the human race. If I am learning golf, horsemanship, electrical wiring, or gourmet cooking, I am very happy for instruction. There is plenty of room for creativity within the rules, but if I step outside the rules and insist on, say, handling live electrical wires, there will be a price to pay for stepping outside the rules! God, in a burst of creative excitement, determined to make a being like Himself who could participate in creation and find the sort of joy and fulfillment He Himself enjoyed. But, of course, there was a right way and a wrong way of such participation. It's not just right or wrong in an arbitrary sense; there was a way that worked and a way that didn't. If we would do it right, we would experience something akin to His own sense of delight. But if not, we could only experience disappointment and ultimately failure and despair.

This will be true of the way we approach everything in our lives, from sexuality to spirituality. We may find some brief excitement in our own illicit approach, but we cannot find fulfillment and joy, and we will eventually find only destruction in doing anything any way other than God's way. That's just the way it is, and the sooner we face that, the happier and the more fulfilled we'll be. We can argue about it, but that seems rather silly when one stops to think about it. It is like complaining that God should have made petroleum taste sweet when He has already made honey. If you want to put petroleum on your toast, fine, but don't complain about the taste. There is an alternative!

Do you see what we are doing when we demand satisfaction from, say, illicit sex? God is pretty straightforward about this in places like Proverbs 5 and 6. Sex, the way I designed it, is sweeter than you can imagine, He tells us. But taking it outside of marriage is a surefire formula for destruction. It's just the way it works. "Can a man scoop fire into his lap without his clothes being burned? ... So is he who sleeps with another man's wife" (Proverbs 6:27, 29). God shakes His head at all our sexual alternatives and says, "But I didn't make it that way. Why don't you try it the way I made it?"

God's intent for us, made in His own image and likeness, was that we would enjoy fully everything He enjoyed. He wanted us to reason, He wanted us to love, He wanted us to create, He wanted us to manage—all in conformity to His generous and enlightening instruction. It was inevitable that when we turned our backs on Him in the Fall and chose to believe in a blatant and ill-disguised lie, all these special human potentialities would be corrupted, and we could no more reflect God's character or enjoy His good creation than we could breathe underwater. We had departed from the very thing we were designed to do, and we could never find satisfaction in that.

THE OFFER OF REDEMPTION

But this was not the end of the story. God knew that to make us with such astonishing potential for good left us open to equally astonishing potential for evil. So He was prepared to seek out His straying sons and daughters and to salvage His fallen creation. The whole of the Bible can be summarized in three words: Creation, Fall, and Redemption. God made us and placed us at the pinnacle of His creation to enjoy it with Him—that's Creation. By our disobedience, we lost our ability to live up to our human potential—that's the Fall. Yet because of His love for us, He has set about to change our hearts and restore our glory—that's Redemption.

Nevertheless, respecting our human freedom and potential, He will not coerce us. He does not take us by the scruff of the neck and force us to love Him. He desires to have a relationship with us, but love must always be chosen or it is not love. Therefore He invites, or perhaps more strongly and more poignantly, He *calls* us to belong to Him and accept the place He has prepared for us. We saw in the previous chapter that the incredible promise of Romans 8:28 that God would work all things together for good in our lives applied, in the final analysis, only to those who in fact love God. Here we find a second qualification for those who would claim this promise. We learn that it applies only to those "who have been called according to his purpose." And what is that purpose? According to verse 29, it is that we "be conformed to the likeness of his Son." Those who have not given their hearts to God to be recast in His image cannot claim the promise that all things in their lives will work out for good.

The idea of God's calling here is also important. It emphasizes God's initiative in drawing us to Himself. The problem is, once we turn away from Him, we are incapable of turning back without His help. We become slaves to sin. We have within us neither the power nor even the desire to return. But God, in His sovereign foreknowledge, determines to reach out to all who will be transformed and to restore God's image in them. He calls us through His Word and through His Spirit at work in our spirits. And that Spirit at work within us actually makes us capable of responding if we will.

It is tremendously reassuring to realize that this is, in the end, God's doing. It does not depend on our inconsistency, our halfheartedness, our lack of discipline, our good intentions neglected. It is God's call, and if it is God's call, then we are encouraged by His declaration through the prophet Isaiah that: "My word . . . will not return to me empty, but will accomplish what I desire and achieve the purpose for which I sent it" (Isaiah 55:11). His purpose is that we would be conformed to the image of His Son, and we may be assured that He will achieve that purpose in us who believe.

We have been using the classic phrase "made in the image of God" to describe His purpose. But the phrase in Romans 8:29 is "conformed to the likeness of his Son." The reason for this change in the wording is important, for in helping us toward the goal of restoring His image in us, God has allowed us to see His Son, who reflects that image perfectly. Hebrews 1:3 says, "The Son is the radiance of God's glory and the exact representation of his being." Jesus Christ came to express God's holiness and love in human form. Colossians 1:15 says, "He is the image of the invisible God, the firstborn over all creation." Paul picked up that same phrase here in Romans 8, where he says we are to be conformed to the likeness of God's Son, "that he might be the firstborn among many brothers" (v. 29). It's a family affair. God wants us to be like our brother, Jesus Christ.

God's plan then is to show us in Jesus Christ just what He had in mind in creating us to reflect His image. We don't really know how we should use our rationality, our relationships, our creativity, our management ability, our morality. He says, "All right, I'll show you." And in Jesus Christ He does just that. We are called to be like Jesus, to think like Him, to love like Him, to live like

Him. We are called to be as rational, as loving, as creative, as effective, and as simply good as Jesus—indisputably the greatest man who ever lived, a man who lived with balance and grace and power and compassion, and who said the secret of His incredible life was simply that He always did the will of the Father. "I do nothing on my own," He said in John 8:28–29, "but speak just what the Father has taught me. The one who sent me is with me; he has not left me alone, for I always do what pleases him."

An example is good, but God also takes into consideration our inability to live up to this standard, even after Jesus' death on the cross has atoned for our sin. So He united us with Jesus Christ by putting His Spirit in all who will receive Him as Lord and Savior. This Spirit at work in the inner man *writes God's laws on our hearts,* the prophet Jeremiah said (31:33), and *moves us to follow His decrees and keep His laws,* according to Ezekiel 36:27. So this is where we have come in applying the promise of Romans 8:28. God makes all things work together for good in the lives of those who have received Christ's Spirit into their hearts and who desire to be transformed by Him.

This, of course, is not an easy task. It will cost something to be shaped in His image. In explaining Psalm 8, the author of the letter to the Hebrews said:

> But we see Jesus, who was made a little lower than the angels, now crowned with glory and honor because he suffered death, so that by the grace of God he might taste death for everyone. In bringing many sons to glory, it was fitting that God, for whom and through whom everything exists, should make the author of their salvation perfect through suffering. (Hebrews 2:9–10)

There is the cost. Jesus Himself was made perfect through suffering. And Hebrews goes on to say, "Both the one who makes men holy and those who are made holy are of the same family. So Jesus is not ashamed to call them brothers" (2:11).

Certainly God may redeem the random violence in our lives. But the implication here is that He quite purposefully uses suffering to deepen and shape us in the image of Christ. He even did it with Jesus Himself! You and I know that the people we really admire, the people with genuine depth of character, are invariably the people who have dealt with great difficulty in their lives. They have not simply whined and complained about all their difficulties, nor sought our sympathy for the injustices they have suffered. Those who are deepened by suffering are those who know they have no warrant to escape the things that trouble others, including our Lord; who see it as a test of their character; and who let God use it to enlarge their hearts and deepen their sensitivity. No one's true character is displayed when everything is going his way. The real test of our character is what happens when things are tough. What emerges when life is difficult and unfair and nobody even seems to care?

BEING LIKE CHRIST

What each of us is called to, in the end, is the imitation of Christ. In writing to the Ephesians, the apostle Paul talked of coming to know Christ. "Surely," he said, "you heard of him and were taught in him in accordance with the truth that is in Jesus. You were taught, with regard to your former way of life, to put off your old self, which is being corrupted by its deceitful desires; to be made new in the attitude of your minds; and to put on the new self, *created to be like God* in true righteousness and holiness" (Ephesians 4:21–24, italics added). That's God's purpose.

This then is our calling, to be conformed to the image of God as we have seen it in Jesus Christ. It will take an effort. Peter challenged us to "be all the more eager to make your calling and election sure" (2 Peter 1:10). Work diligently to prove the claim of Christ on your life, to prove that indeed God has called you and is conforming you to the image of His Son. Thomas Watson said, "If there were a controversy about your land, you would use all means to clear your title; and is salvation nothing? Will you not clear your title here?" You see, the imitation of Christ does not earn our salvation, but it proves it. For after all, either you desire to be like Christ, or you don't. The believer does. The nonbeliever doesn't, not really, not enough to actually work at it.

You and I, then, can claim God's promise to work all things together for our good if we have set ourselves to imitate Jesus Christ. According to the Westminster Catechism, the chief end of man is "to glorify God and enjoy him forever." We reflect His glory when the Spirit empowers us to live as Christ lived. This does not in any way impoverish us. Rather it is the most liberating, enriching life we could possibly imagine. It grants us all the extraordinary privileges and delights we were created to enjoy. And it means that without a moment's hesitation, we can claim the promise that He is directing everything in our lives to an unimaginably good and delightful conclusion.

NOTE

1. J. I. Packer, *Knowing Man* (Westchester, Ill.: Cornerstone, 1979), 24–25.

Chapter Nine

INCOMPARABLE!

Romans 8:17–25

*I*t's very early in the morning, sometime after midnight. You are not sure what has awakened you, but you slowly become aware that you are no longer dreaming. The house is silent, and you are snug under a down comforter—enough to keep an older, wiser child in bed, but you are seven years old, and this could be the best Christmas ever! There were so many special things on your list that the images dance in your head. How long is it till morning? Has that mysterious visitor come and gone yet? One thing is sure: Sleep has escaped somewhere into the night, and now you are stirred by an intense desire for the arrival of daylight.

Can anyone blame you if you slip out from under the covers, tiptoe across the room, and crack open the door? Unable to resist the temptation, a few moments later you are scooting down the carpeted stairs to the first landing, from where you can see partway into the living room. It is dark on the stairs, but from the doorway comes a shifting, exotic light—now blue, fading to yellow, then green, and finally red. An enticing bit of the Christmas tree can be seen from this outpost, and underneath are bright packages in intriguing shapes, decorated with green and red and silver bows. Is that the handle of a bicycle protruding from behind the tree? Your pulse quickens! But a sound from your parents' bedroom suddenly interrupts your reverie, and you scramble back to bed. It's only a few hours till dawn, but it seems like an eternity.

All of us remember when a few hours seemed like an eternity. Anticipation does that! We have been considering an incredible promise of something good to come, a promise anticipated by the very first Christmas when heaven touched us and we received God's greatest gift, wrapped not in silver ribbons but in swaddling clothes and lying not under a tree but in a manger. The promise is that no matter how long the night, no matter how painful the struggle, the God who visited our home on that first Christmas is going to work all things together for good for those who love Him and are called according to His purpose. Indeed, Paul says in Romans 8:18, our present sufferings are not even worth comparing to our ultimate inheritance—what God has called glory.

THE CONNECTION BETWEEN SUFFERING AND GLORY

So what is this glory—the ultimate good toward which God is moving us? Paul tells us in Romans 8:15–17 that God has adopted us into His family and He is working to conform us to the image of His Son so that we might share His inheritance. "If we are children," he says, "then we are heirs—heirs of God and co-heirs with Christ" (v. 17). Then he warns us that there is a condition—"if indeed we share in his sufferings in order that we may also share in his glory." Whatever it is, the road to glory leads through suffering. One reason for this is that something in us makes it impossible to truly enjoy anything that comes without effort. The indulged child upon whom we heap a thousand treasures fiddles with this for a while, and shifts his attention to that, and finally begins to whine and complain that he is bored. By contrast, the person who has long anticipated something seemingly unattainable, who has struggled through repeated disappointments and worked diligently despite the fact that the possibility of achieving that desire seemed remote at best, the person who has paid a price and suffered much in the attempt, will hardly be able to contain his wonder and delight when the goal is actually achieved. God may prepare us through suffering to appreciate glory.

More to the point, perhaps, the apostle Peter, who struggled to live up to his own expectations, wrote, "Therefore, since Christ suffered in his body, arm yourselves also with the same attitude, because he who has suffered in his body is done with sin" (1 Peter 4:1). Here then is a critical way in which suffering works for good:

> As a result, he does not live the rest of his earthly life for evil human desires, but rather for the will of God. . . . Dear friends, do not be surprised at the painful trial you are suffering, as though something strange were happening to you. But rejoice that you participate in the sufferings of Christ, so that you may be overjoyed when his glory is revealed. (1 Peter 4:2, 12–13)

That is a wonderful promise to see you through difficult times. It is the pathway Christ Himself took through suffering to unimagined glory.

Glory we can happily anticipate, but suffering is
another matter. Our more immediate concern about suffering so often preoccupies us and makes us desperate for
the reassurance that God might be able to bring something good out of it. We can hardly anticipate the glory
because we are so preoccupied with the struggle. Here,
however, we learn that suffering is not random accidents
that happened when neither God nor we were paying
attention. Rather suffering is really the means to glory! It's
part of the path. Our Lord's brother James actually said,
"Consider it pure joy, my brothers, whenever you face trials" (James 1:2), because the ability to face those trials leads
to perseverance, and perseverance leads to maturity, making you "mature and complete, not lacking anything" (v. 4).

WAITING FOR GREATER GLORY

Suffering is so much a part of the passageway to glory that Paul suggested we might best compare it to the
birth of a child. There are dark days in the womb, and life
can seem to constrict you so horribly that you become
desperate for release, but then one day it *really does* release
you, and suddenly the pain and trauma of birth doesn't
even seem worth comparing to the glory that is being
revealed.

The fact is, no truly good or great thing comes easily.
If you want "easy," then forget "great" and "good." But
God's goal in all this is to take us beyond these present
struggles to experience glory. And what He begins to
suggest with this word *glory* is beyond our imagination. It
is the glory of the resurrection invading, transforming,
glorifying every aspect of His creation. Nor is it simply
that we get to see God's glory, but that this incomparable

glory is going to be "revealed *in* us"—in other words, we are going to be a part of it!

Romans 8:19 begins to explain where we are in this process. Right now the whole of creation "waits" . . . it's not that way yet. It's the anticipation of Christmas Eve. The whole of creation "waits in eager expectation" for us who are being remade in the image of God to take our proper place of dominion within it—as we were originally created to do. God made us, as we learned in the previous chapter, to have a unique and extraordinary role in His creation. This place of glory that God's Word anticipates is a place where we will finally be properly related to all of creation: the animals, the plants, and the earth itself. Isaiah the prophet anticipated this with his picture of the wolf living with the lamb, the leopard lying down with the goat, the calf and the lion and the yearling together. "A little child will lead them," he said (Isaiah 11:6). The person who truly reflects God's image, loving and caring for His creation, will win, with his care, the very respect and love of that creation.

This idyllic picture contrasts to the present world in which men and beasts prey on each other, but in this new world the predators will be gone: "The cow will feed with the bear, their young will lie down together, and the lion will eat straw like the ox. The infant will play near the hole of the cobra, and the young child put his hand into the viper's nest. They will neither harm nor destroy on all my holy mountain" (Isaiah 11:7–9). The prophet added, "for the earth will be full of the knowledge of the Lord as the waters cover the sea" (v. 9b; see also Habakkuk 2:14).

That is the promise we anticipate—a Paradise free

from the destruction that now reigns, a transformed world that reflects God's glory. Had we taken our proper place within creation in the beginning, this is what it would have been. When, under the influence of God's Spirit, we finally do it, what results will be a glory unimaginable, a world in harmony with God and with those who have finally been conformed to His image. This, then, is the destiny toward which all things are heading for the believer.

THE STRUGGLES OF CREATION TODAY

This all seems quite impossible to us right now because it is so utterly unlike the world we have come to know. We tend to assume this is the only world there could be, but we must keep in mind that this is a fallen world. Nothing in creation is now what God intended it to be. We cannot even imagine the Garden of Eden because, as verse 20 of Romans 8 explains, the whole of creation has been "subjected to frustration"; it doesn't live up to its potential. It is frustrated in achieving anything like God originally intended. And this is our fault. It is not a natural limitation. Human beings made in God's image had a unique and extraordinary place within His creation. Under His authority, we were to have dominion over the rest of creation. But when we rejected God's authority, we brought a curse on the earth itself (see Genesis 3:17), which did not allow it to achieve its original potential. It cannot do what God created it to do.

Furthermore, we humans were banished from God's intended paradise and excluded from access to the Tree of Life. Everything in our fallen world is now, according to Romans 8:21, in "bondage to decay." Everything dies because God has had to limit it until we who were created to steward that creation accept His authority over us. Only then can we be trusted to do within creation what we ought to do. Had God not restricted creation's innate power, we would have abused it beyond imagination! To preserve His experiment, He had to restrict the earth's potential, limit our life span, and ban us from a paradise so bountiful and fecund that, as in Lewis's Narnian Paradise, even a bar from a cast iron lamp post, tossed in the dirt, grew into a lamp! Can you imagine the nightmare of a world filled with such explosive power, controlled by men and women who will not acknowledge God? God chose to restrict it until that day when at least some men and women finally submit to God's will. They alone could be trusted with such an awesome creation. Access to that incredible power by lawless men would be nothing less than hell.

The words "not by its own choice" in Romans 8:20 indicate that the present limitations of nature are not inherent to its design. They have been imposed by God, who may just as easily reverse His action. This revelation addresses the often-asked question, "Why couldn't God have done a better job creating the world?" We see the problems and say, "God could have done better than that." But in fact He did! He did much better than that. It was because of our abuse of power that He had to severely restrict our life span and the life span and productivity of His creation, *until* His true sons and daughters are revealed, at which time "the creation itself will be liberated from its bondage to decay and brought into the glorious freedom of the children of God" (v. 21). The whole of creation is going to be renewed. This is nothing less than a cosmic regeneration. Can you imagine it? God's world liberated to fulfill an unimagined destiny, along with the true children of God!

When we finally realize this, we see that our present pain, and the struggle of the whole of creation, really is best likened to birth pangs as Romans 8:22 suggests. True, it is painful, almost unbearably so—but look what's coming. Birth is the one pain we experience about which we say, "It's worth it!" because of what follows. Our new life will be as advanced beyond the present in its potential as a full-term child is advanced beyond a fertilized egg. That's what's to come. And if you are frustrated with the corruption you still see in the world and in your own life, know that these two millennia since the time of Christ are simply the gestation period. As with any pregnancy, it gets most uncomfortable at the end, just before that exquisite new life emerges.

Not only is this true of the rest of creation, Romans 8:23 says, "but we ourselves" share both the labor pains and the eager expectation of something more—in fact, something infinitely better, something we've gotten a glimpse of through God's Spirit. Having tasted even momentarily His incredible, life-giving power, just the "firstfruits"—those tiny early apples, not yet fully ripe— we can hardly wait to share the fulfillment of God's promise. Then we will experience our adoption as true sons and daughters of our Creator-Father and the glorious transformation of our bodies.

OUR RESURRECTION BODIES

What will our bodies be like in this new creation? John says, "Dear friends, now we are children of God, and

130

what we will be has not yet been made known." But we do know this—"we know that when he appears, we shall be like him, for we shall see him as he is" (1 John 3:2). In those few weeks after His resurrection, Jesus, with His new body, astonished everybody who saw Him. But there was more to come. He asked His followers not to hold Him back, for He was still to return to the Father to be invested with His full glory. We don't know what that involves, but it must be beyond description. And we are going to share it.

What we do know is that the resurrection body will be wholly adapted by God's Spirit, not to the fallen world but to the new kingdom that God is forming. Paul wrote to the Philippians that those who live as enemies of the cross of Christ—who reject God's authority—are living for themselves and for their place in this material world. Thus the perishing world is all they will inherit. "But our citizenship is in heaven," he continued, "and we eagerly await a Savior from there, the Lord Jesus Christ, who, by the power that enables him to bring everything under his control, will transform our lowly bodies so that they will be like his glorious body" (3:20–21). You see, we're going to be like Him! As He brings all things under His control, we will be able to bring our own lives under control, and we will be able to participate in His glory.

It is fascinating to think about what all this means. It must mean that if we are going to be like Jesus, we will no longer be limited by space and time. We will be able to touch the icy fire of stars and explore the whole of His incredible universe. What will be the shape of this new paradise that God is promising, when Creation is freed from its bondage to decay, and you and I find our place within it with transformed bodies and hearts? I am not certain that we are even capable of exaggerating this picture. Certainly it will at least measure up to the various images we have found in the pages of Scripture. We must find ourselves in harmony with an exotic array of wildlife such as we picture in the Garden of Eden. And can you imagine the abundance of flowers and fruits and trees when the curse on the earth's productivity is lifted? "Now," God says, "you'll see what I made this earth capable of doing!" Rivers, no longer polluted by our abuse, choked with algae, or muddied by storms, will flow "as clear as crystal." Imagine lakes and oceans where you can see all the way to the bottom. And imagine the light. As much as I love the sun, the Bible says we won't need it anymore. Far better, light will radiate from God Himself, almost a liquid light you could bathe in, shimmering and iridescent, a light only suggested now on a crystalline morning as the sun creeps over the horizon and brings a new day to life, or when, settling onto the mountains, it bathes the landscape in warm, golden splendor. Light is a beautiful thing, but when we see the light from the very face of God, it will take our breath away.

Set free from our own bondage to aging and decay, I suspect we will be in a condition to enjoy this world in a way we can only dream of now. We will be able to see with the eyes of eagles. We will be able to hear the songs of the birds and the insects. We will have bodies that will not weaken through exercise but will get stronger. When Isaiah said we will "mount up with wings as eagles . . . run, and not be weary . . . walk, and not faint" (Isaiah 40:31 KJV) he meant literally that. Can you imagine bounding up a mountain for the view and not feeling breathless at the top? Our power and energy always building and never diminishing! That is the way God intended it to be.

OUR HOPE AND ANTICIPATION

Best of all, we will find this to be our True Home. We will have finally arrived at the place where we belong. We shall not feel like aliens and invaders who have stumbled across some place of beauty that we can only appreciate momentarily as a spectator. We won't get so used to the view we won't see it anymore. Nor will we find our enjoyment troubled by the nagging reminder that this glorious day must eventually end. No, we will find that we have come to the place where we belong. Remember that morning when you were a child in school, and you woke up, and the sun was shining, and you realized it was the first day of vacation, with the whole summer still ahead of you? When we arrive in God's glory it will always be that first day; everything still lies ahead.

It is to this ultimate hope and expectation that we are saved, Romans 8:24 says. God is offering us infinitely more than we presently have. That is why we call it our hope of glory. "Who hopes for what he already has?" Don't compare it to what you already have, He says. "But if we hope for what we do not yet have, we wait for it patiently" (v. 25).

You might think what we have said here is rather silly, wishful thinking. You may think it is too good to be true. But to you I would say on the contrary, it is too good *not* to be true. How could we possibly imagine a world that's better than God is capable of making? Whatever we imagine—it must be even better than that! Whatever He has in store for us, it is all this at least and much more. Christians should decidedly *not* be content with the things of this earth, nor should we be intimidated by those who scoff at a "pie-in-the-sky" mentality. Should we settle for less? Does our God want us to settle for less than the best He is capable of sharing with us? God has promised us an incomparable glory—the highest fruition of all He originally intended, superseding even the Garden of Eden, which, after all, was never intended to be more than an entryway into the kingdom of God.

So we are challenged to continue in anticipation, but to do so patiently, for God is not finished with us yet, nor is He finished with our world. In all things, however, as we have learned, He is continuing to work in us to prepare us to become a part of that final glory. Any suffering we go through here simply stretches us. It enlarges our capacity to receive and to enjoy all the unimaginable wonders He has in store. The apostle Paul reminded us of this incomparable promise in his letter to the Corinthians, "Eye has not seen, nor ear heard, nor have entered into the heart of man the things which God has prepared for those who love Him" (1 Corinthians 2:9 NKJV).

So I must leave you with that question: Do you love Him? Do you desire to be with Him more than anything else in the world? Because if you do, this promise is yours!

THE PROCESS

Chapter Ten

THE BANKRUPT

HEART

Romans 3:9–12,
19–20; 7:13–25a

*O*ur hearts long for the incomparable glory discussed in the previous chapter, and we can imagine that the road to glory might be long and difficult. But for those who take it seriously, the most devastating, perhaps the most terrifying thing is the realization that even in the best of times, our hearts are decidedly *not* fixed on God's glory. If this promise is to those who love God and are being conformed to His image, we may well begin to despair. For our own lives are marked by failure and outright rebellion. How can we claim the promise that all things will work together for good when the reality of our lives is a daily battle with sin that we seem to lose more often than we win?

Perhaps it would be helpful to look at the true story of a remarkable and talented young man who, by anybody's reckoning, was destined for success. Born into a fine family, he developed early into the sort of person everybody should have known would one day make a name for himself. As a youth he demonstrated remarkable self-discipline and was willing to take on significant responsibilities. As he matured, he grew into a ruggedly handsome young man with a powerful, athletic body and an artistic temperament. One of those people who "had it all," he learned to play several musical instruments, sang beautifully, and composed moving, lyrical poetry. His charismatic personality, coupled with his extraordinary courage, soon won him wider acclaim. After a brief but tremendously successful military career, the dashing young officer moved into politics. By the age of thirty he had risen to the highest position in the land.

Although he certainly encountered difficulties along the way, his life was marked by an astonishing string of successes—and the recognition, wealth, and power that came with it. He enjoyed great popular support, was married to a particularly bright and beautiful woman, and if that wasn't enough, he demonstrated a bold and inspiring faith as well. In fact, he was so good and so successful that even though people couldn't help but admire him, some found themselves resenting him at the same time.

But at the pinnacle of his career, this young man stumbled, and stumbled badly. The most popular leader his nation had known, his job approval rating soaring, he began to believe that he was above the law. Arrogance and self-indulgence led him into an adulterous relationship. When circumstances threatened to expose him, he attempted a cover-up that ultimately involved him in the death of his illicit lover's husband. For a little while it looked as if he might get away with it, but then a trusted adviser confronted him. And the man, whom you know as David, the most popular king in Israel, was devastated by this failure. He couldn't believe what he had done. He couldn't believe that he, David, who had always prided himself on his integrity and his high moral standards, who walked so closely with the Lord, who composed those beautiful psalms, could fall so low.

And David's sin had serious consequences—for him, his family, and his country. But David, to his credit, faced up to his sin. He genuinely humbled himself, repented and accepted God's discipline, and then went back to his work a chastened and a wiser man. "I know my transgressions," he wrote, "and my sin is always before me. Against you, you only, have I sinned and done what is evil in your sight, so that you are proved right when you speak and justified when you judge.... Hide your face from my sins and blot out all my iniquity" (Psalm 51:3–4, 9). He went on to pray, "Create in me a pure heart, O God, and renew a steadfast spirit within me. Do not cast me from your presence or take your Holy Spirit from me. Restore to me the joy of your salvation and grant me a willing spirit, to sustain me" (vv. 10–12). You hear David's heart pleading with God in this prayer to maintain his communion and to cleanse his soul once again. Then as he considered what God might require of him, the sacrifices he might bring, he concluded, "The sacrifices of God are a broken spirit; a broken and contrite heart, O God, you will not despise" (v. 17).

We all long for success, but success leads to pride, and I'm afraid that unbroken success leads straight to hell. As much as we desire it, success is not really what we need. What we really need, as David saw, is to be broken. The only thing of value we can bring to God is a broken and contrite heart. If we are not broken, we will never come to recognize our need for God and give ourselves fully to Him. So this is the primary way in which sin and failure might work for something good in our lives.

David had been very successful, but success had led him into a dangerous spiritual pride from which only a strong dose of failure could save him. Hot-tempered and self-serving before his failure, his brash arrogance now began to mellow into compassion and generosity and genuine humility. During his son's attempted coup some time later, he was moved to tears by the generosity and love that others offered him. He had felt entirely self-sufficient before; now he began to appreciate others. Recognizing how undeserving he was of all that God had given him and everything his friends had done for him, he became less harsh and judgmental of others and more quick to forgive.

And he began to see his responsibility as a leader in an entirely new light. He realized that his calling as king was to be a servant to his people—not to ask them to serve him. When it was time for his son to succeed him on the throne, he offered the moving and humble advice we have come to know as the last words of David. "He that ruleth over men must be just, ruling in the fear of God. And he shall be as the light of the morning, when the sun riseth, even a morning without clouds; as the tender grass springing out of the earth by clear shining after rain" (2 Samuel 23:3–4 KJV). David *was* like the sun rising out of the mist on a cloudless morning for his people, but not before he had learned, through his own failure, that he was weak and needed to depend upon the Lord for his strength daily.

How God Uses Our Worst for His Best

We have been talking about how God works all things together for good for those who love Him, who are called according to His purpose. In this chapter we want to explore how God uses even our worst sins and failures to accomplish good in our lives, and David is Exhibit A. I know something personally about David's humiliation and its effects. Perhaps you do too. All of us are susceptible. The better we know that, the better we might guard against some devastating failure. But even if we stumble and fall, God wants to use that failure in our lives. Surprisingly, He doesn't want to use it to beat us over the head and tell us how terrible we are. He wants to use it to shape us in His image. We will hardly admit our failures to ourselves, let alone to one another. But God says, I want to use your sin and your failure to shape you in the image of My Son, Jesus Christ. I can use it to make you able to enjoy all that I want to give you. "If we claim to be without sin, we deceive ourselves and the truth is not in us. If we confess our sins, he is faithful and just and will forgive us our sins and purify us from all unrighteousness. . . . My dear children, I write this to you so that you will not sin. But if anybody does sin, we have one who speaks to the Father in our defense—Jesus Christ, the Righteous One" (1 John 1:8–2:1). It is not the only way God can work, and He certainly does not will our failure or our sin, but failure can be the motivation for setting a whole new course in our lives that may lead us to heights we would never have achieved without it.

Americans at the beginning of the twenty-first century suffer from a near fatal blindness. We seem unable to recognize sin. This is astonishing. If there is one thing that is indisputable in our world, it is the reality of sin—which G. K. Chesterton called "the only part of Christian theology which can really be proved." "Whether or no [a] man could be washed in miraculous waters," he mused, "there was no doubt at any rate that he wanted washing."[1] But we won't admit there is anything wrong in our lives. In Psalm 103:14 David, the man who had learned from his failure, said about God, "He remembers that we are dust." David himself had forgotten that he was merely dust, that he was susceptible to failure. He forgot that only God's Spirit within us stirs us to life, that we are not gods who can choose our own way with impunity. He forgot that our only opportunity for life and joy is in submission to the way God has designed. Death will ultimately destroy our petty claims to be our own gods, of course, and we will return to the dust out of which we were made, but by then it will be too late. One of God's graces is to allow us to come face-to-face with our fallenness. If we are willing to learn, this can provide a wake-up call while there is still opportunity to make things right.

We think we are pretty good folks. Romans 3 is a scandal in our postmodern world. "There is no one righteous, not even one; there is no one who understands, no one who seeks God" (Romans 3:10–11). Well, we say, that's pretty harsh; I seek God, after all, and I know a lot of good people. But that is precisely the sort of thinking the apostle is addressing here. *As long as you think you are good, there is no hope for you.* We live in a world that continually tells our children, "You are fundamentally good." The goal may be commendable, but

God's Word says, no, before you can build self-esteem, you must realize that you are fallen.

> Now we know that whatever the law says, it says to those who are under the law, so that every mouth may be silenced and the whole world held accountable to God. Therefore no one will be declared righteous in his sight by observing the law; rather, through the law we become conscious of sin. But now a righteousness from God, apart from law, has been made known. (Romans 3:19–21)

God alone is good. We are not. If you see no need for God to purge your soul and transform you, you are lost and there is no hope for you. That is why it is absolutely essential that we recognize sin.

In fact, God says here, that's why I have given you the Law. It wasn't just a list of things you ought to do—you already know what you ought to do. What I want is for you to look honestly enough at the Law to see that it does not describe you. The Law describes goodness—absolute, uncompromising goodness. It describes God, not you. Jesus tried to make that clear in the Sermon on the Mount. He says, "You have heard in the Law, 'Do not murder' and 'Do not commit adultery.' I'm telling you that doesn't describe *you* if you let your heart fill with anger or with lust. You see, the Law really serves only one significant purpose" (paraphrase). Romans 3:19–20, quoted earlier, says the Law is intended to silence that sort of talk. What the Law does is show us that we don't measure up. "Through the law," the apostle Paul wrote, "we become conscious of sin" (v. 20). The law then, as it describes a perfect righteousness attainable only by God, serves us chiefly by making us aware of our own sinfulness.

But this turns out to be tremendously important. It is like a diagnostic test by which we may learn of a potentially fatal disease harbored in our body. If you have such a disease you had better know about it! In Romans 7 Paul showed us precisely what happens in us when we are confronted with a law. I read once of a whimsical sign that read, simply, "It is forbidden to throw stones at this sign." In all honesty, what does that statement make you think of doing? *You think about throwing stones at the sign!* That sign reveals something inside yourself that you weren't necessarily willing to admit. A resort hotel built out over the water had a serious problem with glass being broken by people attempting to fish from the windows, despite the fact that every window contained a sign reading, "Please do not fish from the windows." Someone who understood human nature solved the problem by simply removing all the signs!

Paul said in Romans 7, "I would not have known what coveting really was if the law had not said, 'Do not covet.' But sin, seizing the opportunity afforded by the commandment, produced in me every kind of covetous desire" (vv. 7b–8a). The Law did just what it was intended to do. It told me what I ought not to do, and right away my heart began to desire what was forbidden. The Law wasn't bad. I even concede that the Law states what I ought to do. But the moment I encounter a law, my sinful heart begins to rise up in rebellion. The moment someone tells me what I ought to be doing, I don't want to do it. The Law, then, enables us to recognize sin. Sin leads inevitably to death. Unfortunately, all of us harbor sin in our hearts. Like any fatal disease, if we don't acknowledge it and deal with it, it will destroy us. So God's first goal is to get us to recognize sin in our lives.

SEEING THE SIN IN OUR OWN LIVES

Two different categories of words in the Bible describe sin. One category has to do with falling short, failing to measure up to some standard. Until we are faced with a stark failure, we have a tendency to deceive ourselves into thinking that we have it within us to measure up to God's standards. Until we really give it a serious try, we don't realize we are not going to make it. So sin and failure give us a more realistic assessment of ourselves. The second category of words for sin has to do with deliberately trespassing a boundary. This is not just falling short, not quite being strong enough or courageous enough or insightful enough. This is where God says, "Don't go there!" and we look Him in the eye and step across the line. This sort of failure reveals to us that we are fundamentally rebels at heart and need to be humbled before we can be renewed, before God can make anything good out of our lives.

If we ever learn to recognize sin in our lives, it eventually leads us to a startling and, I'm afraid, very disquieting revelation about ourselves. We eventually realize not only that we occasionally fall short, or even that we deliberately disobey at times, but that we have become nothing more than slaves to sin. We couldn't get away if we tried. This is a horrible realization. It is like the person who begins to experiment with drugs and finds that he is addicted—now he cannot escape, and suddenly all his hopes and dreams begin to crumble before his eyes. But, you see, all sin turns out to be addictive. None of us know this until we have tried our best to escape. If you don't know that you are addicted to sin, you haven't really tried to escape. Try it seriously, Paul says, and you will find that you are a slave. Once again, this is a terribly significant revelation if we are ever to deal effectively with our sin.

This is stated powerfully in Romans 7:13–23. With a withering honesty, Paul here described what he found out about himself when he finally resolved to do better. "I do not understand what I do," he said, the shock evident in the passion of his words. "For what I want to do I do not do, but what I hate I do" (v. 15). I hope you have felt that way. If you have, you have begun to be honest with yourself. Obviously, Paul concluded here, a power at work within me drags me down toward failure and death, even when my desire is to do what is right and good. Until we recognize there is something evil at work within us and we are slaves to this sin, we are not going to get any better!

Most of us will deny this for a long time. It is, after all, a devastating discovery to learn that we are slaves to sin. We want to believe that we can do the right thing if we want to. It is a terrifying thought that sin might be so rampant in our lives that we could not escape its deadly clutches no matter how hard we try. We refuse to think it. We will not believe this about ourselves—until at last every attempt to clean up our lives has been met with yet another devastating failure and we finally find ourselves alone and hopeless. It is what every true saint has called "the dark night of the soul"—the realization that we have nothing good inside. "I know that nothing good lives in me," Paul said (Romans 7:18).

It is at this, the lowest and most hopeless moment in our lives, that we are finally faced with the most significant choice we can ever make. Recognizing the futility of our resistance, we can do either of two things: We can despair and succumb to the sin that will ultimately destroy us, or we can despair and surrender to the One who can ultimately rescue us from sin's fatal grasp. We have both options. In Romans 7, Paul chose the second option. "What a wretched man I am!" he says. "Who will rescue me from this body of death?" (v. 24). I can't get away from my own body, but it is contaminated with sin and destined for death. "Who will rescue me?" he asked. And then he announced his surrender to Jesus Christ as Lord. It is in this surrender alone that we are saved.

SEEING OUR FAILURES AS GOD DOES

God works all things together for the good of those who love Him, we are told, and this promise applies to those "who have been called according to his purpose" (Romans 8:28). We explored that purpose and found it was to be conformed to the likeness of God. "Those he called," Paul explained, "he also justified; those he justified, he also glorified" (v. 30). God works through our sin and failure to bring us to our knees where He can finally justify us, or remove our guilt. What is required is that we confess our sin and surrender our lives to Him, as David did. But we will not do it until we know the dilemma we are in. That grand offer of freedom from the otherwise fatal consequences of sin can only be received by those who actually acknowledge their sins and, like a drowning man, cast themselves upon Him for rescue.

This is why the recognition of our susceptibility to failure is critically important. As the title of this chapter suggests, our fundamental problem is our moral bankruptcy. This is what Paul wanted to make sure we saw in Romans 7. If we don't know we are bankrupt, we will keep writing checks on an empty account until the law catches up with us. We have nothing but moral liabilities. The only moral assets belong to Jesus Christ. Our only hope, therefore, lies in His offer to cover our debts and make us heirs to His fortune. That is what justification is all about.

We began by asking if there is any way God can use our sin and failure and accomplish something good. We were not asking if He could simply salvage the wreck of our lives, but if even our failure might contribute in some substantial way to our becoming more Christlike. Although we deeply regret our failures and know we must often live with the consequences, we would like to know that in God's economy He can actually take our sins and build us into something better than we might have been—that we need not be paralyzed by past failure, but might be able to rejoice in the way God uses it for good. The story of David shows us an astonishing array of blessings that we may enjoy if we are willing to learn from our failures.

LESSONS TO BE LEARNED FROM FAILURE

Let us end by summarizing the lessons David learned, and we might learn, from failure. It is a remarkable and encouraging list, twenty-five ways God uses failure for our good:

1. *We see ourselves more realistically and honestly.* Nothing can improve in our lives until we begin with a realistic self-assessment.

2. *We realize how capable of evil we really are*—a harsh

but necessary lesson if we are ever to surrender ourselves to Christ.

3. *We become more aware of our destructive passions and our pride, less trusting of our own wisdom and strength.*

4. *We learn humility, which weans us away from pride,* the one sin which, if it is not checked, leads directly to hell. It is the sin of pride that made the devil the devil.

5. *We recognize how little we are giving to God.* Before we fail, we often think we are giving God much more than we actually are.

6. *We are driven to seek communion with God,* which we tend to neglect when we think things are going pretty well.

7. *We become more open to hear what God desires to tell us about ourselves and about Himself.*

8. *We become more deeply desirous of holiness and glory.* If we really see our sin for what it is, we begin to desire something better.

9. *We become less judgmental of others* when we realize how vulnerable we personally are to sin.

10. *We become more sensitive and sympathetic toward the weak,* more willing to spend our energy lifting others when they have fallen.

11. *We begin to look up to people instead of looking down on them,* an important change in perspective that comes from recognizing our own failure.

12. *Our souls become more submissive and more obedient.* We are more pliant when we recognize our failure.

13. *We depend more on God and the power of His indwelling Spirit—less on ourselves.*

14. *We become more dependent on prayer.* We get on our knees when things have gone wrong, more rarely and less intensely when things are going right.

15. *We welcome the support and prayer and even the counsel of others.*

16. *We take sin more seriously, recognizing its addictive nature and its destructive power.*

17. *We are forced to rethink our priorities and to practice the disciplines that might strengthen us.* When things are going well, it is so easy to get priorities out of order and to neglect essential habits of self-discipline.

18. *We learn perseverance the hard way—which is the only way anyone can learn perseverance.* We learn tremendously important lessons about getting up and going on so failure will not paralyze us. The only fatal error is not to get up again when we have fallen.

19. *We learn meekness.* Meekness essentially involves leaving our defense to God. Failure encourages us to stop trying to convince everyone of our righteousness.

20. *We learn something of the depth of God's grace and compassion toward us.* In Jesus' moving parable of the Prodigal Son, the elder brother, who had not yet recognized his own failure, could not appreciate his father's compassion. But the Prodigal could. When you and I recognize our sin, we begin to recognize the incredible love that God has for us. He doesn't beat on us for our sins. Like the Prodigal's father, when we acknowledge our sins, He opens His arms and says, Come back to Me; I want to love you.

21. *From that we may learn to respect and love ourselves more appropriately.* I doubt that we can ever love ourselves until we really believe that God loves us.

22. *In our emptiness we are prepared to receive God's fullness.*

23. *We allow God to purge our souls with the necessary firmness,* which we would resist if we felt we did not

deserve it. Ridding our lives of sin requires a severity that we are virtually unable to summon on our own strength, particularly if we think there is any other way.

24. *We take Satan more seriously, having experienced his enslaving power.*

25. *We learn to surrender to God, who alone can deliver us from evil.*

Sin is a terrible thing, but we may be tempered by failure, and in the process we become more honest, more compassionate, and more committed to Christlikeness. If we lament the irretrievable loss of innocence and opportunity represented by our sins, perhaps this little sonnet penned by the old Scottish preacher and writer George MacDonald might be an encouragement. As an old man who has learned something in his life, he writes in *Diary of an Old Soul,*[2]

> Lord, what I once had done with youthful might,
> Had I been from the first true to the truth,
> Grant me, now old, to do—with better sight,
> And humbler heart, if not the brain of youth;
> So wilt thou, in thy gentleness and ruth,
> Lead back thy old soul, by the path of pain,
> Round to his best—young eyes and heart and brain.

NOTES

1. G. K. Chesterton, *Orthodoxy: The Romance of Faith* (New York: Image, 1959), 15.
2. George MacDonald, *Diary of an Old Soul* (Minneapolis: Augsburg, 1994), 10.

Chapter Eleven

REFINED

BY FIRE

1 Peter 1:3–9

*O*f all the chapters in this book, this has been by far the most difficult to write. The question is, How may God work for good through our suffering and loss?—a wrenching question that has haunted the human family from the beginning of time. What has been written in response to the question tends to be either theoretical or agonizingly personal. I must say at the beginning that I write more from the first perspective than from the second. I readily admit that I am not an expert on pain and suffering, nor do I wish to become one.

I have only been brushed by tragedy a few times in my life. My young brother was killed in a plane crash one fine Christmas Day. He was my only brother, and I grieved then the loss I still feel today. But the pain was far more intense for my parents. Perhaps the greater loss was watching the light fade from my father's eyes.

Others will have felt the sharp thrust of pain more personally, at that vulnerable point where all theories are challenged. Yet I would speak first of all from God's revelation in His Word, second from experiences told to me either in person or in writing by those who have suffered more severely, and only last from the few personal experiences that seem to confirm what I have been told. Perhaps some small objectivity will be helpful here, though I most want to avoid the arrogant blindness of Job's friends.

Besides, while there is no doubt a legitimate fraternity of persons who have experienced profound loss, the fact is that most of us must learn to deal with the smaller but perhaps no less threatening losses that plague us all in this broken world.

HOPE FROM TRAGIC LOSS

Gerald Sittser, a professor from Whitworth College in Washington state, was driving with his family in a minivan when it was struck head-on by a drunken driver traveling at a high rate of speed. The accident killed his mother, his wife, and his four-year-old daughter—three generations in one crushing blow! This we all recognize as a catastrophic loss, the sort of horror we read about in the news and shudder to imagine happening to us. But, as he pointed out in *A Grace Disguised,* while his may have been a more spectacular loss, uniquely painful losses happen to all of us all the time. Someone we love is diagnosed with Alzheimer's or a terminal illness. An accident or injury leaves us with a permanent disability. We become the victim of a crime. We suffer physical or emotional or sexual abuse. A child's world is shattered by the announcement of his parents' divorce. A pink slip informs us that the job we have held for twenty-six years has just been terminated. A fire or flood destroys not only our home and security, but the relics of a lifetime of treasured memories. Months slip into years and we are unable to conceive a child. Or a long-awaited child is born with severe birth defects. All these losses are devastating. The future we had anticipated dissolves and blows away in the merciless wind. We wonder how we will cope. The thought that something good could ever come from such losses seems naive at best; at worst it seems absurd—beyond hope.

And yet the promise we have been examining from Romans 8:28 suggests this is precisely what God intends to do. "And we know that in all things God works for the good of those who love him, who have been called according to his purpose." We must not say this glibly. It is small consolation to one who has just had a loved one torn away, perhaps violently and unnecessarily. Nevertheless, the promise is God's, not ours, and however wrenching may be my pain, I want to believe it is true.

Different Responses to Suffering

We can, perhaps, imagine this with lesser ills. Our lives are filled with relatively minor pains and disappointments every day, from which we learn important lessons in patience and perseverance. But if our normal losses are like a broken limb from which we may expect to fully recover (perhaps becoming even stronger at the broken places), other losses are of such magnitude that they are like an amputation. One does not recover from an amputation. We may heal, but things will never be the same. Whether through divorce or death or mental illness or another traumatic experience, our husband or wife or child or parent or friend is gone. Our hopes are gone, our opportunities are gone, our dreams are gone. The results from this sort of loss are permanent and cumulative. Nor can catastrophic losses be mitigated by replacements. Another spouse, another child, or another life cannot erase the former loss. It becomes an indelible part of our experience. And our question is, How could any such pain or loss serve a good end?

All of us see some people who are enlarged and deepened by suffering and others who are destroyed by it. What makes the difference? You and I need to know, because we face losses as well. It is easy to become paralyzed with fear or depression or guilt. Many become bitter or jealous and are consumed with anger at the injustice of suffering. Some become obsessed by a desire for revenge. Others become entrapped by despair and self-pity. All these reactions may be at least partially justifiable. But justifiable or not, what they have in common is that they are all equally debilitating. They all ensure that our suffering will shrivel and ultimately destroy us.

God's promise to take even our most terrible losses and accomplish something good with them applies only to those who, because they have learned to love and trust Him, choose a different response. Although we cannot choose the circumstances of our lives, we *can* choose how we will *respond* to the circumstances of our lives. That is one of the most important things we can learn from suffering. We did not audition for our particular role in the drama of life, but we may choose how we will play the role.

You may not have chosen to suffer a head injury, a divorce, infertility, or the loss of a job or a child, but you are responsible for how you *respond* to that loss. And it is your *response,* not the incident itself, that will determine who you become—whether you are enlarged and deepened, or whether you are shriveled and destroyed by your loss.

If we will accept the pain and continue to trust God in the midst of it, how might He take suffering and loss in our lives and work it together for good, as He promised? What good could possibly come from such devastating and dark losses? One of the great stories of Scripture is that of Joseph, a favorite son who early on enjoyed all the privileges of love and favor. But those advantages began to shape Joseph into a self-centered braggart who alienated everyone around him. His brothers' jealousy drove them to sell him into slavery and convince his father that he was dead. Joseph, who might have been embittered by that event, was somewhat subdued. Forced to look at life without all the privileges he once thought were his due, a chastened Joseph nevertheless kept his faith and sought to live uprightly, doing his best under very difficult circumstances.

For a time this course of action served him well, and he rose to a position of prominence in his master's home. But then tragedy struck again. When his master's wife failed in her attempt to seduce him, she falsely accused him of attempted rape and he was thrown into prison with no hope for the future. Here again Joseph might have become bitter and vengeful or allowed himself to be consumed with self-pity or despair. But instead, once again he made the best of his circumstances, eventually capturing the attention and trust of the prison master and through him gaining a position of responsibility even there. A favor done to a prominent fellow prisoner ought to have been returned but was forgotten, an injustice that left the young man in prison for two more years. Eventually, however, it led to his release and elevation to one of the highest political offices in the land. From there, as you know, he became instrumental in saving his family from starvation in a devastating drought, and ultimately preserving the entire race of God's people.

Joseph, who had maintained his trust in God through some seventeen years of injustice and loss, later observed to his brothers, "You intended to harm me, but God intended it for good" (Genesis 50:20). And indeed, on at least two levels God was working the circumstances of Joseph's life for good. First of all, he himself grew to a greatness he could not have achieved without going through the losses. Suffering made Joseph the great leader he became. In addition, God was at work behind the scenes accomplishing an even greater good in the salvation of His people. The difference with Joseph, as with us, lay in his *response* to the suffering that intruded so unfairly into his life.

Nearly every person with whom I have ever walked through a tragedy raises the question Joseph might have raised, the question of the seeming unfairness of our losses. The question is unavoidable, and yet, legitimate or not, what I have seen is that all who grow from suffering must, like Joseph, get past the sense of injustice that will otherwise paralyze them. The fact is that although we bring some bad things on ourselves and sometimes we cause each other pain, other things just happen to us, as they have to all people at all times. Those who grow through their suffering recognize that the question is not really "Why me?" It might as well be "Why not me?"

Further, they come to realize that, if they are fair in their estimation, a predominance of good things happen to them also, and these they do not deserve any more than the bad.

In this way some who have suffered the greatest losses come to appreciate the good things in their lives that were taken for granted before their suffering. People who grow through their suffering consistently say they come to appreciate friends and loved ones more than ever before. Some begin to look at the world with eyes that have been opened by that pain to recognize normal sights and sounds and smells—the way the sunlight is refracted through beveled glass, or the ringing of a distant church bell, or the smell of baking bread—as works of exquisite, almost painful beauty given them to enjoy.

Gerald Sittser, the professor who lost members from three generations of his family in a car accident, leaving him to rear the three surviving children alone, talked about being overwhelmed by how wonderful ordinary life came to seem after his initial trauma and despair. "Simply being alive," he wrote, "became holy to me. As I saw myself typing exams, chatting with a student on the way to class, or tucking one of my children into bed, I sensed I was beholding something sacred."[1] And it is true. Life is sacred. The world is filled to overflowing with God's incredible masterpieces. But we may not notice or appreciate them until our senses have been honed by pain. God may use suffering to awaken us to the beauty of life in the present moment. Sittser tells of finding himself savoring an almost intolerable beauty in things like the reflection of the moon on new-fallen snow. It was as if the same experience that had made him so terribly vulnerable to pain had ironically made him exquisitely sensitive to beauty as well. Can those who have never known suffering truly recognize splendor?

AWARENESS OF WHAT'S VALUABLE

Certainly it is also true that God may use suffering in our lives, if we will allow Him, to wean us away from the shallow and superficial things that demand so much of our attention, and force us to focus instead on Him and on what is truly important. Pain and loss can give a clarity and focus to our lives that is almost impossible in the midst of the clutter and distraction of our normal routine. After losing her thirty-four-year-old husband to a brain tumor, my sister spoke almost wistfully of the intensity and focus of her life in those final days as she cared for him at home and watched him disengage from their tiny son. There was, she said, a tangible presence of God that she expected she would not feel again this side of heaven. Important things leapt into focus while extraneous things faded away.

The awareness that things can be taken away in a moment challenges us to spend more time and energy on what really matters. Consistently, those who have been deepened by adversity say that they have come to realize how precious are the relationships they are privileged to have. Before the loss they may have spent minimal time nurturing those relationships or they may have let petty grievances come between them. But the deep pain of personal loss awakens them to the tremendous value of opportunities to love someone.

Indeed, loss may increase our capacity to love. Somehow love becomes more authentic when it grows out of our brokenness. Too often, we are only seeking to satisfy ourselves. Pain may, if we will allow it, help us to set aside our pride and our natural desire to serve ourselves and begin to appreciate how others, too, might be hurting. We may become more able to see the good and the courageous and the noble in others when our eyes have been opened by pain. When we are full of ourselves, we hardly notice or care about another's pain. But in our brokenness we may find ourselves sensitized to the pain that surrounds us.

In this way pain opens our eyes to the enormous suffering in our world—something we may have done our best to ignore before we felt the hurt ourselves. In that pain we may be moved beyond our normal self-indulgent complacency to become genuinely involved in the lives of others. Dave Dravecky, former all-star pitcher for the San Francisco Giants who lost his throwing arm to cancer, says the loss moved him away from a preoccupation with his own needs and began to teach him compassion for others. As a result, he began a ministry of encouragement to others who have suffered losses, a ministry that has blessed thousands. "If I'd have continued on as a ballplayer and missed that," he says, "*that* would have been a tragedy."[2]

Another way God may bring good out of our suffering is by stripping away our pretense and our vanity. Suffering gets us down to the heart of things. Walking through a painful experience can help us do the right thing for the right reason. Some react angrily and use pain to justify immoral behavior or selfishness. But those who let God speak to them through pain find themselves learning to do the right things for the right reason. We may spend time with friends, for example, not because we feel obligated, but because we truly value their friendship. We may do the right thing not from a weary sense of duty, but because somehow it seems more important in the light of genuine suffering. Pain or loss moves us to consider what we are doing, to take a careful inventory of our lives and to do what we do on purpose. We can't just expect that a comfortable and good life will happen to us. We need to take control of our lives. Rather than simply taking the path of least resistance, we may begin to do what we do on purpose. We become more intentional in shaping our lives to be what we ought.

In this way loss can be transforming in our lives. By waking us up to the ways in which we were living somewhat aimlessly, and allowing us to see the importance of our behavior and the seriousness of our ends, pain can motivate us to break bad habits that we have ignored for years. It can motivate us to cultivate new behaviors and to set good and clear goals for our lives. Don Hoak, the great third baseman for the Pittsburgh Pirates, during his military service experienced the death of his brother, who was killed in action as they moved forward in battle. From that day, Hoak decided he had two lives to live, one for himself and one for his brother. The result was an intensity and drive that enabled him to accomplish a level of greatness he would likely never have achieved without the loss.

People who have suffered great losses are often overwhelmed by the selfless love and generosity of others. They have said to me, "I don't know if I would have done for anyone else what they've done for me." The result is often that they are drawn out of their isolation and begin to allow others to become involved in their lives. Certainly this is closer to what God had in mind for us from the start.

Most of us live most of our lives under remarkably favorable circumstances. Thus when we do finally encounter loss, it strips bare our treasured myth of self-sufficiency and we begin to realize how weak and vulnerable we really are. If we are paying attention, the insufficiency of our response to pain also dawns upon us. As we see our own anger or depression or self-pity, we begin to see something of the feebleness, perhaps even the ugliness of our own souls. Initially, this may depress us further. But God wants to use it to draw us to Himself. Often it takes an experience that faces us with our weakness and mortality to move us to recognize our utter dependence upon God and to seek a relationship with Him. A young woman in our congregation discovered, at age twenty-nine and newly married, that she had a cancer that would take away her ability to have children, if not her life. Yet she said, "I need that hole in my life to keep me focused on Him." It was the incident that turned her life around and brought her into a rich and rewarding relationship with God. When it is time to deepen, nothing is quite so effective as suffering.

DRIVEN TO GOD

Only in communion with our Creator can we experience the hope and promise that supersedes our grief and loss. If we don't come to the God who ultimately conquered death itself, where will we go? Tragedy pushes us toward the God we are prone to ignore when things are comfortable.

We may come reluctantly, but what we discover here is truly profound. At first, driven to God by our own inadequacies, we may only resent Him. We may feel very little love if we see ourselves as nothing more than pawns in the hands of a sovereign and inscrutable God. But what we ultimately find is the astonishing truth of the incarnation. Nicholas Wolterstorff lost his son in a climbing accident in Austria. In a terribly poignant book entitled *Lament for a Son,* Wolterstorff went through the awful questions that such a loss raises for us—questions about the goodness and sovereignty of God and about our own ability to continue with the business of living. Most of the questions are never answered. But what *does* happen turns out to be far more significant than a theoretical answer to our question. "Instead of explaining our suffering," he writes, "God shares it."[3] He was finally comforted by the simple fact that God knows what it is like to lose a Son.

Sittser said that in the three years since his family was killed he has never once sat through a communion service without tears. And the reason is that he began to understand what communion is all about. The God we at first accused of being responsible for our suffering, since He alone might have prevented it, turns out to be a God who comes to share our suffering. He makes Himself helpless, placing Himself at the mercy of merciless forces. Although He might have exercised His power to escape, He chose not to. Instead He walked through the very vortex of suffering in order to identify with us, to demonstrate His love for us, and to conquer our final enemy, Death itself. Those who suffer always appreciate the person who is willing to set aside his privilege and come and suffer with them. Of course, that is precisely what God did.

What God ultimately desires to do in our lives through suffering, as we learned earlier, is to shape us in the image of Christ. Jesus Himself, God's Word says, was shaped by suffering. But if we too are to be shaped, we must not resist the fire or the anvil and the hammer, painful as they may be. This is not to say that we must welcome suffering. Even Jesus asked the Father if He might be spared. But to be spared all pain would be to lose the one great benefit that might have come—the opportunity to be shaped in the image of Christ. Those who become bitter and angry instead of becoming malleable in God's hands never learn the deeper joys, the acute sensitivity, the clearer focus, the sense of participation in the truly momentous affairs of God's universe—lessons they might have learned had they let God walk them through their pain.

In the end, we must understand that if God is going to equip us to enjoy the delights of His universe, then He must enlarge our souls. We simply do not have the capacity to take in His delight and His glory. So our souls must be stretched in order that we might receive what He wants to give. The very things that make us capable of experiencing joy are the same as those that make us capable of experiencing sorrow. If we did not truly love someone, we would not experience grief at his death. Wolterstorff, after losing his son, wrote, "Love in our world is suffering love. Some do not suffer much, though, for they do not love much. Suffering is for the loving. If I hadn't loved him, there wouldn't be this agony. . . . In commanding us to love, God invites us to suffer."[4] The more fully and the more acutely we love, the more expansive and the more acute will be our grief. But the opposite is true as well. When God stretches our souls to embrace sorrow, He is in fact enlarging our capacity to experience true joy and delight.

At the climax of his book, Gerald Sittser confessed:

> I still want [my family] back, and I always will, no matter what happens as a result of their deaths. Yet the grief I feel is sweet as well as bitter. I still have a sorrowful soul; yet I wake up every morning joyful, eager for what the new day will bring. Never have I felt as much pain as I have in the last three years; yet never have I experienced as much pleasure in simply being alive. . . . Never have I felt so broken; yet never have I been so whole. Never have I been so aware of my weakness and vulnerability; yet never have I been so content and felt so strong. . . . What I once considered mutually exclusive—sorrow and joy, pain and pleasure, death and life—have become parts of a greater whole. My soul has been stretched. Above all, I have become aware of the power of God's grace and my need for it.[5]

In his first letter, the apostle Peter explained, "Now for a little while you may have had to suffer grief in all kinds of trials" (1 Peter 1:6). Yes, but there is a purpose in all this. "These have come so that your faith—of greater worth than gold, which perishes even though refined by fire—may be proved genuine" (v. 7). If your faith is genuine, then the promise of Romans 8:28 is yours.

This is not a question of loving a God who only abuses us. It is a question of trusting a God who has in fact given us abundant evidence of His love, most fully in

Jesus Christ. It is a question of loving Him enough and trusting Him enough to let Him have His way with us, no matter how painful it is; like our old collie dog, who got a little too curious about a porcupine, letting my dad remove a score or more of barbed quills from her nose and mouth. It is a painful process, but one done in love. If you and I will let God refine us, in that act He will remove all the impurities that would have kept us out of heaven itself, so that one day He will be able to usher us into that "inheritance that can never perish, spoil or fade —kept in heaven for you" (1 Peter 1:4), a place of unimaginable glory, as we learned in chapter 9.

That place, of course, has been secured, as Peter tells us, by the resurrection of our Lord Jesus Christ. And if we stop and think about it, the resurrection is the single gift that can restore all losses and redeem all suffering. Without the resurrection those catastrophic losses would indeed be amputations from which we could never recover. But in the resurrection even the worst possible loss is restored. Anything, then, which brings us into the embrace of the God of resurrection is of inestimable value —even our greatest pain.

NOTES

1. Gerald Sittser, *A Grace Disguised* (Grand Rapids: Zondervan, 1995), 36–37.
2. Dave and Jan Dravecky, *When You Can't Come Back* (Grand Rapids: Zondervan, 1992), 195.
3. Nicholas Wolterstorff, *Lament for a Son* (Grand Rapids: Eerdmans, 1987), 81.
4. Ibid., 89.
5. Sittser, *A Grace Disguised, 179–80*.

Chapter Twelve

OUT OF
THE SILENCE

Isaiah 64:1–12

Sooner or later it will be our turn, darkness spreading a pall over everything we have cherished, our hopes crushed, a dull ache gripping our soul, and then, worst of all, when we cry out to God for help—a vast, impenetrable silence! How can we possibly continue when the heavens mock us?

C. S. Lewis, a man of great faith, felt this silence when his wife died. He wrote very honestly about it in a little book called *A Grief Observed*. Listen to what happens even in a godly man's soul when God is silent.

> Meanwhile, where is God? This is one of the most disquieting symptoms. When you are happy, so happy that you have no sense of needing Him, so happy that you are tempted to feel His claims upon you as an interruption, if you remember yourself and turn to Him with gratitude and praise, you will be—or so it feels—welcomed with open arms. But go to Him when your need is desperate, when all other help is vain, and what do you find? A door

slammed in your face, and a sound of bolting and double bolting on the inside. After that, silence. You may as well turn away. The longer you wait, the more emphatic the silence will become. There are no lights in the windows. It might be an empty house. Was it ever inhabited? It seemed so once. And that seeming was as strong as this. What can this mean? Why is He so present a commander in our time of prosperity and so very absent a help in time of trouble?[1]

It is not great sinners who are troubled by the silence of God. They weren't listening anyway. It is the great saints who know the devastation of God's withdrawal. "How long, O Lord? Will you forget me forever?" David wrote in Psalm 13:1a. "How long will you hide your face from me? How long must I wrestle with my thoughts and every day have sorrow in my heart? . . . Look on me and answer, O Lord my God. Give light to my eyes, or I will sleep in death" (vv. 1–3). David reached this point more than once in his lifetime. "Save me, O God, for the waters have come up to my neck" (Psalm 69:1), he wrote in words that Jeremiah the prophet might have quoted when that fate befell him later. "I sink in the miry depths, where there is no foothold. I have come into the deep waters; the floods engulf me. I am worn out calling for help; my throat is parched. My eyes fail, looking for my God" (Psalm 69:2–3). You sense the anguish, the desolation, the feeling of being abandoned. "To you I call, O Lord my Rock; do not turn a deaf ear to me. For if you remain silent, I will be like those who have gone down to the pit" (Psalm 28:1).

Whether or not you and I have found ourselves in such a pit, how often have we wondered why God, if He exists, does not speak to us more directly and perform some of the spectacular miracles recorded from ancient times? At a time when faith languished, Isaiah wrote:

> Oh that you would rend the heavens and come down, that the mountains would tremble before you! As when fire sets twigs ablaze and causes water to boil, come down to make your name known to your enemies and cause the nations to quake before you! For when you did awesome things that we did not expect, you came down, and the mountains trembled before you. Since ancient times, no one has heard, no ear has perceived, no eye has seen any God besides you, who acts on behalf of those who wait for him. (Isaiah 64:1–4)

Isaiah longs for a God who speaks and acts in vivid and powerful ways in our world. We reason with Isaiah that if God were more visibly present in our world, He would inspire greater faith, and we would find it easier and more compelling to obey and to do His will. But would we? Look more closely at what happened when God did come down. In Exodus 19:18–19 we read an awe-inspiring account of Mount Sinai "covered with smoke, because the Lord descended on it in fire. The smoke billowed up from it like smoke from a furnace, the whole mountain trembled violently, and the sound of the trumpet grew louder and louder. Then Moses spoke and the voice of God answered him." Just what we wanted, right? Ah, but the people shrank away. As we learn in the next chapter, they said to Moses, "Speak to us yourself and we will listen. But do not have God speak to us or we will die" (20:19). That's their response to an audible voice from God. Moses replied that God was testing them to see if the fear of God would keep them from sinning.

But did it? "Everything the Lord has said we will do," the people promised Moses (Exodus 24:3), but before he got back from the mountain, they had made an idol for themselves and danced themselves into an orgiastic frenzy around it. So much for their resolve to obey this highly vocal and visible God! Is it guidance you want? I will be a pillar of cloud by day and of fire by night, directing every step of your pathway through the wilderness, God had told them. And the next thing you know, God was saying, I want you to go in there, and they refused to go. So then God said, Well, in that case don't even think about going there or you will be defeated by your enemies, so they immediately got up and went and were defeated by their enemies! So much for a God who guides every step of our path.

You want a God who will take care of your every need? He was there providing water from a rock and manna in a barren desert, and all the people would say was, "What are you trying to do, kill us out here in this desert? We remember the 'chef's special' back at *The Sphinx,* fish and cucumbers, melons, leeks, onions and garlic" (see Numbers 11:5).

And it wasn't just that generation. No revival followed the spectacular display of God's power on Mount Carmel when fire fell from heaven at the word of the prophet Elijah and consumed the sacrifice, the altar, and the water the people had poured on it. And after all Jesus' astonishing miracles, witnessed by thousands, He had all of 120 followers left when He returned to heaven. The stunning fact is that spectacular evidence of the presence of God has never had much of an impact on anyone's faith. That tangible evidence we long for, those miraculous demonstrations of power that we believe the world would understand and obey, have historically made little or no difference. There is no reason to believe it would be different with us.

OUR EXPECTATION THAT GOD WILL EXPLAIN

Nevertheless we continue to demand that God explain Himself to us, as if the potter owes the clay an explanation. This was Job's demand in the face of his awful suffering, and we sympathize. If God wanted him to suffer that way, at least He should be there explaining Himself. "Though I cry, 'I've been wronged!' I get no response," Job complained (19:7). "If only I knew where to find him; if only I could go to his dwelling! I would state my case before him and fill my mouth with arguments. I would find out what he would answer me. . . . [But wherever I go] I catch no glimpse of him" (23:3–5, 9).

Job did eventually hear God's response, but he did not get his questions answered. Essentially God said to him, "Job, I am under no obligation to explain Myself to you, and even if I did, you would not be able to understand. You simply need to know that I am God." It would be well for us to remember that we too are in no position to demand anything from God, and besides, His universe is so complex and His ways so inscrutable that it is doubtful the explanations we demand would do us very much good.

Nevertheless, it does seem to us that we could find some compromise here. Of course God is sovereign; we are willing to acknowledge that. And of course we are puny, dependent creatures with a limited grasp. But it was God who made us in His image after all, with an ability, however limited, to relate to Him. And this is not how *we* treat people. If we cannot give a comprehensive explanation to a small child, we nonetheless offer some words of comfort and an explanation on a level he *can* comprehend. Could not God do the same for us?

IS GOD REALLY SILENT?

But I wonder, has God really been as silent as we accuse Him of being, or is the problem that we have not *honestly* listened? Perhaps we do not *really* want to hear what He has to say. On the contrary, we often want Him to respond like an indulgent parent, "Yes, yes, my dear, whatever you say!"

Isaiah acknowledged that our sin can be one of the causes for that distance between us. Along this line, God gave a simple answer for His silence through the prophet Zechariah: "When I called, they did not listen; so when they called, I would not listen" (7:13). There it is. What parent has not said: "Why do I even bother talking to you? You never listen to me!" All through the Scriptures we find God desiring a relationship with us, but at the same time we find us consistently ignoring His initiatives. Is God *really* silent, or are we just not listening?

The fact is, God *has* spoken. Should He arrive as fire on the mountain, what would He say that He has not already said—either in His Word, in the Word become flesh in Jesus Christ, or through the stirrings of His Holy Spirit in the inner person? We complain about God's silence, but again and again those *willing* to hear pick up His Word and meditate on it, even in the deep anguish of their souls, and find that there *is* a response, and it is very personal and very compelling.

Yet, in all fairness, this silence isn't only due to our

sin. Even the greatest saints have experienced the "dark night of the soul" when nothing relieves the pain, when the words remain on the page no matter how many times they read them, when no one seems to be listening no matter how often they cry out in prayer, when they have no clear direction and no assurance of support, when it is dark and they are alone and the horizon is bleak, and they can see no hope for the future and no resolution to their dilemma. What then?

You and I need to be reassured that even in the silent times, God is working for good in our lives. Even when He seems distant, He is taking the circumstances of our lives and accomplishing something good. I would like to suggest that through God's silence, we may learn to do three significant things. In His silence God can help us to grow up, learn to love, and grow strong—stronger than we ever could have imagined. Remember, the promise that "all things work together for good" is guaranteed to those who love God, who are called according to His purpose—to be shaped in the image of Jesus Christ. In Ephesians 4:13, the apostle Paul spoke of God's goal that we grow up, that we "become mature, attaining to the whole measure of the fullness of Christ"—in other words, conforming to His image. "Then," he explained, "we will no longer be infants, tossed back and forth by the waves, and blown here and there by every wind of teaching and by the cunning and craftiness of men in their deceitful scheming. Instead," he concluded, "we will in all things *grow up* into him who is the Head, that is, Christ" (vv. 14–15, italics added). Don't ever lose sight of God's goal that we will get past the infancy stage and grow up into the image of Christ.

THE GOOD PARENT

So how does a good parent help children mature and grow strong? Well, think about it. How do children learn to walk? Or swim? Or ride a bike? They learn these and other skills when we take away our hands! Let me contrast a good and a bad parent. Perhaps in this comparison we will see that we have been asking God to be a bad parent.

I knew a man who was born with no arms. But this handicap was offset by the fact that he was also born with a very wise mother. He tells the story of the day when she and a neighbor stood watching him, a toddler, rolling on the floor and crying and trying to pull his shirt over his head with his feet. Finally the neighbor could stand it no longer. "Why won't you help him?" she cried. His mother looked her in the eye and replied, "I *am* helping him!" Today that man lives a normal life, dressing himself, eating, even writing with his feet. And he is grateful to his mother for helping him by taking away her hands!

By contrast I knew another parent who never blessed her son with silence. She told him everything she wanted him to know and to do. He was never allowed to be on his own or to make his own decisions about anything. Even when he was a teenager, she laid out every article of clothing for him every morning. At age fourteen, most of this young man's friends were seven or eight years old. He was the most helpless, immature young man I have ever met in my life. And we shouldn't wonder, for how do children grow up? They grow when their parents step back at appropriate moments and allow them to function on their own. The parents don't go away. They are still there to provide counsel and love and a network of security, but they stop giving constant directions, and allow—sometimes even force—the child to make up his own mind, to do it on his own initiative, to take some risks and to live with the consequences. If the goal is growing up to maturity, then the child needs to become less and less dependent.

In her little book *The Liberty of Obedience,* Elisabeth Elliot reflected on the fact that God hasn't answered all of our questions as He might have. She wrote:

> It appears that God has deliberately left us in a quandary about many things. Why did He not summarize all the rules in one book, and all the basic doctrines in another? He could have eliminated the loopholes, prevented all the schisms over morality and false teaching that have plagued His Church for two thousand years. Think of the squabbling and perplexity we would have been spared. And think of the crop of dwarfs He would have reared![2]

Essentially, this is what happened to Israel in the wilderness. On our earlier theory, hearing God's voice regularly and seeing His acts of power, they should have become people of enormous and effective faith. But what happened? Their faith was, if anything, more puny and fickle than our own. They hadn't grown at all. Again and again they showed themselves to be infants in their faith.

Directions and support are vital, of course, but the constant intervention serves us primarily during our "infancy." Eventually we have to take those directions and jump in and try to apply them ourselves. It's like learning to swim or learning to rappel down the face of a steep cliff. The instructions are fine at the outset; we need them, but we never learn until the instructor takes his hands away and steps back and we have to go it on our own. So with our lives, God often stays quite involved with young, immature Christians. But as we grow and mature, He increasingly withdraws from us. One might have thought it would be the other way around. In the beginning we think, *When I mature as a Christian, I'll be able to hear God's voice better and I'll be closer to Him.* We thought we would see more of God, but it must be the opposite or we will never become capable of the things He desires from us.

It is essential to this goal of "growing up" into maturity in Christ, then, that we proceed from the context of God's silence. Of course we still have His Word, but often we lose that sense of His constant presence, His Word loses its urgency and immediacy for us, and we have no sense that He intends to explain Himself. You see, He wants us to follow His counsel because it is best for us and will lead to a good end, but He wants us to be able to *see* the wisdom of His counsel and *choose* to follow it, not because we have been forced to, but because we have learned to desire it in our hearts as Jesus did. Only when this change has taken place within us will we have become mature and Christlike.

GOD'S WOOING

If gaining wisdom and self-discipline, learned best in the crucible of firsthand experience, is the first goal of growing us into the image of Christ, the second goal is to develop within us the *desire* to do God's will. We can know more than anyone who has gone before us, but our knowledge is irrelevant until we choose to put it into practice. The desire to do God's will grows from two fundamental bases. We must learn to love Him, and we must learn to trust Him, our final two points. Having stepped back so we may learn to launch out in the strength He has given us, God's next goal is to win our love.

And here once again, it will not do for Him simply to overwhelm us. As C. S. Lewis says, "He cannot ravish, he can only woo." God could force Himself upon us by overwhelming us with His presence and power, but love is never won by force. Instead, God chooses to "romance" us. He sends us invitations to the dance; He does not drag us in by our hair. There is wisdom in what we often call "playing hard to get." We can hardly respect, let alone truly love, someone who follows us around like an abandoned puppy. It is when we realize that our potential lover may not be there if we do not take some initiative that we begin to take loving seriously! God knows that, and it is true in our loving relationship with Him as well.

So once again, I think God sometimes says, "Hey! You've got My number. Call if you're interested. I'm going to be out enjoying My friends." You might be offended and say, "Let Him go. What kind of a god is that?" But in turn He says, "Well, now I know her heart." Our hearts are not revealed if He only forces Himself upon us. Our hearts are revealed when we express our desire for Him.

In the end, God not only wants us to grow up and to love Him, but He wants us to grow strong and bold and good. If we are ever going to be all God created us to be, the last and greatest thing we will have to learn is to trust

Him implicitly. How do we learn to trust? The great psychologist Paul Tournier says, "Where there is no longer any opportunity for doubt, there is no longer any opportunity for faith either."

Once again, then, we learn to trust God when He ultimately withdraws from us and we must act without seeing Him. Our faith is not tested when God is close and everything is clear and comfortable. Nor do we grow under such circumstances. Faith grows when we must act in the darkness, sometimes again and again as the darkness increases, finding God faithful only after we have faced the ultimate test and still refused to quit.

This seems harsh, but it is, after all, precisely what Jesus Himself suffered. The greatest anguish of the Cross was not the intense physical pain, but the awful sense in the midst of that pain of having been abandoned by God. Remember those haunting words from Psalm 22:

> My God, my God, why have you forsaken me? Why are you so far from saving me, so far from the words of my groaning? O my God, I cry out by day, but you do not answer, by night, and am not silent. Yet you are enthroned as the Holy One. . . . In you our fathers put their trust; they trusted and you delivered them. They cried to you . . . and were not disappointed. (vv. 1–5)

Psalm 22 was quoted by Jesus while He still retained the power to end the experiment and remove Himself from the cross. No voice came from heaven then. Only the silence of a universe that seemed to mock His faith as those gathered at the foot of the cross ridiculed Him: "He trusts in God. Let God rescue him now if he wants him" (Matthew 27:43). The ultimate test of faith is the request that we obey when there is no visible reason for obeying.

Jesus, whom we are to be like, suffered this test, but perhaps none of our fallen race has had to face the test as Job did. That story has captivated us for generations because, without any clue as to what was taking place, Job first lost his livelihood, then his children, then his health (suffering from painful boils over his entire body). Then he lost even the respect of his community and the sympathy of his friends. The only thing left was his faith. His wife, fed up with a God who would not honor her good husband, continually urged him to abandon that.

Job went through unbelievable anguish and was quite understandably upset with God (who never actually faulted him for this). But what you find in that book is that Job never relinquished his faith: "Though he slay me, yet will I hope in him" (13:15). In Job's mind, God was on trial here for His fairness—which is what you and I usually have in mind when we challenge God to speak. But in the book of Job we know, since we've gotten a peek behind the curtain, that in fact it was not God who was on trial, but Job. Satan had observed, quite perceptively, that in the truest sense, you cannot call it pure faith as long as there are rewards. To some extent, Job's trust was self-serving. Pure faith would be trusting in the person of God without any rewards—trusting God simply because He is God. Satan said to God here, "Your experiment with humans is a failure. No one will serve you without a bribe. Faith is a fiction. Take away the reward and even your best exponent will fail." And God said, "OK, he's in your hands."

NAKED FAITH

What you and I learn from the story of Job is that, in the end, the only thing that can prevail against evil is what we might call *naked faith*. If it is a matter of rewards, then evil usually has the advantage. Don't you ever say to yourself, *Why do I keep doing this? I know what's happening. I know I'm being deceived*. Even when you know what is wrong, the short-term rewards are so compelling. And here is one of the most critical points any of us will ever reach in our Christian walk. All of us, I believe, reach a ceiling in our growth that cannot be transcended until we finally let go of rewards and simply say, "I will do this because God said it; I will do this because it is the right thing to do. He doesn't have to give me any more reasons. He doesn't have to promise me anything. I'll do it because God said it." This commitment, if we can make it, catapults us into a level of achievement and a level of experiencing God's delight several orders of magnitude above the level most of us now inhabit. If we are ever to know the fullness of God's riches, it must come to us through naked faith.

One of the inspiring insights we might gain from Job's story is an awareness that we are, each of us, involved in a cosmic drama. Job didn't know that. He thought he was just sitting on an ash heap with a couple of friends. He didn't know that you and I were watching! The angels in heaven were watching. Generations past and to come were watching. When the book of Hebrews tells us that we are surrounded by a great cloud of witnesses, it suggests a stadium of cosmic spectators gathered to see how you and I will handle the testing of our faith. When difficult things happen to you, you think you are on your own and it doesn't matter a whole lot to the world how you respond. Not true! The book of Job reveals that a cosmic drama is going on and every one of us is a part of it. Small victories will be met by polite and courteous applause. But think about the real heroes! Think of a hero led into the arena, and then, before the eyes of saints and angels, handicapped—deprived, perhaps, of weapons, blindfolded, maybe even chained before facing the ultimate contest. The spectators gasp and glance anxiously at one another. A vast, breathless quietness descends upon the stadium. How could any contestant prevail against such odds? The universe is watching!

Then, suddenly, the aggressor is released and bounds in for the kill like a wolf attacking a wounded prey. At the first strike, perhaps, our hero falls to his knees, stunned. He leaps to his feet, alert, tense, anticipating the next charge. Perhaps the scene is repeated again, and then again. But finally, summoning up all his strength and courage and wisdom, he remembers the only weapon that, in the end, can defeat evil in this unequal combat. It is that naked faith of which we spoke a moment ago. Uttering a prayer for help, he poises, moves, recoils in the imposed darkness precisely as he has been trained to do by the Master—even though he cannot see. And by this act of blind faith he ultimately outwits and finally defeats his enemy. The stands erupt in paroxysms of applause! What an incredible display of raw faith and power!

One of Jesus' disciples, Thomas, a good man and honest, refused to enter the arena blindfolded. He insisted on seeing. That's fine, Thomas, Jesus allowed, but there are some genuine heroes coming along after you without any of your advantages. "Blessed are those who have not seen and yet have believed" (John 20:29). He may have been referring to you, one of the true heroes yet to come!

Perhaps the most powerful insight of Lewis's *Screwtape Letters* is in chapter 8 where he described what is going on when Christians are called to persevere when every support to their faith has been withdrawn. Listen to the warning of the senior tempter to his junior. (You will recall that good and evil are reversed here; the "Enemy" is God.)

> You must have often wondered why the Enemy does not make more use of His power to be sensibly present to human souls in any degree He chooses and at any moment. But you now see that the Irresistible and the Indisputable are the two weapons which the very nature of His scheme forbids Him to use. Merely to override a human will (as His felt presence in any but the faintest and most mitigated degree would certainly do) would be for Him useless. He cannot ravish. He can only woo. . . . He is prepared to do a little overriding at the beginning. He will set them off with communications of His presence which, though faint, seem great to them, with emotional sweetness, and easy conquest over temptation. But He never allows this state of affairs to last long. Sooner or later He withdraws, if not in fact, at least from their conscious experience, all those supports and incentives. He leaves the creature to stand up on its own legs—to carry out from the will alone duties which have lost all relish. It is during such trough periods, much more than during the peak periods that it is growing into the sort of creature He wants it to be. Hence the prayers offered in the state of dryness are those which please Him best. . . . He wants them to learn to walk and must therefore take away His hand; and if only the will to walk is really there He is

pleased even with their stumbles. Do not be deceived, Wormwood. Our cause is never more in danger than when a human, no longer desiring, but still intending, to do our Enemy's will, looks round upon a universe from which every trace of Him seems to have vanished, and asks why he has been forsaken, and still obeys.[3]

It happened at the Cross. Job managed it also. Perhaps the next applause from the cosmic stadium will be for us!

NOTES

1. C. S. Lewis, *A Grief Observed* (New York: Seabury, 1961), 9.
2. Elisabeth Elliot, *The Liberty of Obedience* (Waco, Tex.: Word, 1968), 56–57.
3. C. S. Lewis, *The Screwtape Letters* (New York: Macmillan, 1982), 38–39.

Chapter Thirteen

THE TOUGHEST THING

YOU'LL EVER FACE

Philippians 4:4–20

Throughout this book we have seen all the good things God can bring out of bad in our lives. He can use suffering and silence and even sin with astonishing effectiveness to accomplish good and beautiful things in our lives. But none of these things, not pain, not violence, not injustice, not even death can begin to approach God's most remarkable achievement. In fact it is rather easy to see how *failure,* for example, improves us by causing us to strive more diligently and seek the help we need. It is easy to see how *pain* can help us avoid destructive behavior and become more sensitive to those who suffer. It is equally obvious how *emptiness* and lack of fulfillment in our lives can move us to seek God's face. These are good things growing out of something bad. But we have not yet spoken of something that has ruined more people than all these evils combined, something that has brought down kingdoms and turned good men and women onto evil paths and destroyed happy and healthy relationships.

What I am talking about is the challenge of abundance in our lives, or perhaps to spell out the danger more clearly, *the peril of prosperity.* We do not generally think in these terms, but prosperity is perilous to our spiritual health. Many people have grown and deepened and achieved true nobility through difficult circumstances. Few have survived affluence.

Look at the record. If anybody ever had all the advantages, it was King Solomon in the Old Testament. Not only was he wealthy beyond imagination, but he was also healthy in a time when health could not be taken for granted, he was renowned for his wisdom, and he lived in a time of unparalleled prosperity and security. He had the admiration and respect of nearly everyone who knew him and was surrounded by beautiful and talented people. God was with him, and he was successful in all his undertakings. And what was the result of all those blessings? We might have expected all those things to work together for the greatest possible good in his life. But that was not the case. Instead his wives, that wealth, and perhaps the pride he felt in his wisdom conspired to bring about his downfall and the division of his kingdom into two petty kingdoms destined to destruction.

It is not an isolated case. Second Chronicles 26 tells the story of King Uzziah's success and prosperity. "His fame spread far and wide," we are told, "for he was greatly helped until he became powerful. But after Uzziah became powerful, his pride led to his downfall" (vv. 15b–16). A later king, Hezekiah, was also prosperous and successful. He became critically ill and asked for one of the good things we constantly pray for—health. But the chronicler records, "Hezekiah became ill and was at the point of death. He prayed to the Lord, who answered him and gave him a miraculous sign. But Hezekiah's heart was proud and he did not respond to the kindness shown him; therefore the Lord's wrath was on him and on Judah and Jerusalem" (2 Chronicles 32:24–25). Here again is one of God's good gifts, but the effect was negative in Hezekiah's life.

It was precisely the concern about which God had issued some of His sternest warnings as His people stood poised to enter the Promised Land after so many years of struggle in the wilderness. "Be careful," God had warned in Deuteronomy 8,

Remember how the Lord your God led you all the way in the desert these forty years, to humble you and to test you. . . . Know then in your heart that as a man disciplines his son, so the Lord your God disciplines you. . . . [But now, he says, if you think all those hazards in the desert were a problem, now] the Lord your God is bringing you into a good land—a land with streams and pools of water, with springs flowing in the valleys and hills; a land with wheat and barley, vines and fig trees, pomegranates, olive oil and honey; a land where bread will not be scarce and you will lack nothing; a land where the rocks are iron and you can dig copper out of the hills. *When you have eaten and are satisfied, praise the Lord your God for the good land he has given you. [But] be careful that you do not forget the Lord your God.* . . . Otherwise, when you eat and are satisfied, when you build fine houses and settle down, and when your herds and flocks grow large and your silver and gold increase and all you have is multiplied, then your heart will become proud and you will forget the Lord your God, who brought you out of Egypt, out of the land of slavery. . . . If you ever forget the Lord your God and follow other gods and worship and bow down to them, I testify against you today that you will surely be destroyed. (vv. 2a, 5, 7–14, 19, italics added)

I want to bless you, He was saying, but understand that blessing is going to be a severe trial—your greatest yet. And of course as God anticipated, Israel could not survive the perils of prosperity. The recurring refrain of God through prophets like Jeremiah, Ezekiel, and Hosea was: How could you do this? I loved you like My own son; I delivered you from slavery, and cared for you all those years in the wilderness; I brought you into a land flowing with milk and honey, and how have you responded? You have become proud and turned your back to Me. Ezekiel says, "The splendor I had given you made your beauty perfect, declares the Sovereign Lord. But you trusted in your beauty and used your fame to become a prostitute" (16:14–15). The more I did for you, God suggested through Hosea, the further you went from Me. You see, they were not well served by God's blessing.

THE BIGGEST DANGER IN WESTERN CULTURE

No, the fact is, abundance and prosperity have brought down many an empire, from Babylon to the present day. Indeed, the connection between prosperity and the onset of destruction is so apparent that when the psalmist laments, "Why do the wicked prosper?" I am tempted to answer, "Well, perhaps because God has already given up on them!" He allows them to prosper because they are already beyond hope. If He thought there was a chance to redeem them, perhaps He might spare them the curse of abundance. Abundance is a severe test, and few have suffered it successfully. One who is truly concerned about godliness may wisely desire to avoid abundance.

In his magnum opus *How Should We Then Live?* Francis Schaeffer wrote of the two impoverished values that would spell the demise of Western culture, "personal peace" and "affluence." Personal peace he defined as the desire to be left alone to enjoy one's own life, not having to be troubled by other people's problems. Affluence he defined as "a success judged by an ever-higher level of material abundance." But these twin values are false gods that distance us from the true God, from each other, and even from ourselves. Prosperity is destructive if it makes us believe we have no need for God. It is destructive if it isolates us from others, if it dilutes our sense of compassion or destroys our initiative, if it feeds our pride and our complacency. And prosperity has a tendency to do all these things. How many people have we seen whose character has atrophied over abundance? It is more of a curse than we would like to admit.

In a recent election, one presidential adviser coined the phrase: "It's the economy, Stupid!" meaning that's all that counted. But it wasn't! It was, and continues to be, self-indulgence and lack of self-discipline that erases the names of presidents from the annals of the great men and women of history, that destroys careers, marriages, and finally the souls of those who might, under worse circumstances, have become people of genuine faith and character. We are tested more by prosperity than by adversity.

Thus when the apostle Paul said in Philippians 4:11b–12, "I have learned to be content whatever the circumstances. I know what it is to be in need, and I know what it is to have plenty. I have learned the secret of being content in any and every situation, whether well fed or hungry, whether living in plenty or in want," thoughtful observers will respond in awe, "Now *that is* remarkable! If he can deal with abundance, he has survived his greatest challenge." I know people can grow from being abased; I know people can deepen from suffering want. But is it really possible that God can *even* bring something good out of the *good* things in our lives? For the fact is, the toughest thing any of us will ever face in our lifetime—the one thing that is more likely than anything else to destroy us—is not adversity, but abundance.

WHY GOD TAKES THE RISK OF BLESSING US

In his *Screwtape Letters,* Lewis has the senior devil advise his junior tempter:

> If [a man's] years prove prosperous, our [Satan's] position is even stronger. Prosperity knits a man to the World. He feels that he is "finding his place in it," while really it is finding its place in him. His increasing reputation, his widening circle of acquaintances, his sense of importance, the growing pressure of absorbing and agreeable work, build up in him a sense of being really at home on Earth, which is just what we want . . . for the difficult task of unravelling their souls from Heaven.[1]

So here, it seems, is the supreme test for the God who promises to bring good out of "all things" in our lives. Clearly we face serious risks from the blessings in our lives. So what good can God bring from these good gifts? This is not an exhaustive list, but let me suggest a few reasons God may think it is worth the risk to bless us.

First of all, through the good things He brings into our lives, the Lord expresses His great love for us. In Deuteronomy 7:8 God says, "It was because the Lord loved you ... that he brought you out with a mighty hand and redeemed you from the land of slavery." And then he added:

> If you pay attention to these laws and are careful to follow them, then the Lord your God will keep his covenant of love with you, . . . He will love you and bless you and increase your numbers. He will bless the fruit of your womb, the crops of your land—your grain, new wine and oil—the calves of your herds and the lambs of your flocks in the land that he swore to your forefathers to give you. You will be blessed more than any other people. (vv. 12–14)

God was saying, I love you and want to express it by prospering you. "Every good and perfect gift is from above, coming down from the Father," James reminded us in the New Testament. Because of His love, God risks giving us good things.

So through blessings like family, health, and abundance, God lets us know we are loved. And it's worth the risk because we need to know. The gifts of the bridegroom express his love and secure the relationship between him and his bride. And of course, this is the Ultimate Good toward which God is working in our lives. If He can secure for us a closer relationship with Himself by blessing us with abundance, then that is what He will do. However, He knows our hearts, and if that Ultimate Good can better be achieved through privation, then that is what He will do—again because He loves us. Either way He is motivated by love. His goal is to achieve that enriching relationship with Him for which we were made. Will abundance and prosperity nurture that relationship? Or will adversity and privation?

A second possible good that may come to us through prosperity is the building of self-confidence. It is difficult to maintain confidence when all we experience is failure. The way God dealt with Gideon in the Old Testament book of Judges is instructive here. When God called Gideon, the timid young man was found hiding in a winepress. Told that God wanted him to lead his people against the invading Midianites, Gideon responded, "How can I [do that]? My clan is the weakest in Manasseh, and I am the least in my family." But God answered, "I will be with you, and you will strike down all the Midianites together." You see, it isn't really about us. It is about what God wants to do through us. As Paul says in Philippians 4:13, "I can do all things *through Christ* who strengthens me" (NKJV, italics added). And of course, that is the basis for true self-confidence. We can't fail if Christ is working through us. So our confidence increases when we see God accomplishing good things in our lives.

It is worth noting that the greatest self-confidence grows out of dependence upon God, not, as we may have thought, out of what we accomplish independently. The reason is that we were designed for God to express His power and glory through us. Paul wrote to the Ephesians, "I pray that out of his glorious riches he may strengthen you with power through his Spirit in your inner being" (3:16). Obviously the power of God operating in us far transcends any truncated human abilities. So our greatest confidence comes when we experience God at work in us. Through such successes, God builds our self-confidence and introduces us to true self-esteem, which is humble respect for the things God chooses to do through us.

I grew up on the prairies of western South Dakota, where cattle ranching was one of the primary occupations. One of the most fascinating things to watch was a horse and rider who were particularly adept at "cattle-cutting." The idea was to isolate a particular animal from the herd and keep it out until it could be dealt with separately—no small job in dealing with a herd animal that immediately becomes desperate to rejoin its kind. A good "cutting horse" was astonishing to watch. It could wheel and spin like a ballet dancer, keeping its nose on a darting calf as if it could read its mind and sprinting to keep its body between the determined exile and the rest of the herd.

The horse was great! But of course without his rider and trainer, the horse was just a horse, running with its own herd, grazing whenever it felt like it, utterly unable to achieve its own potential! We are the same. We can't begin to tap our own human potential until God begins to express His will through us. We may be self-satisfied—presumably the untrained horse is—but genuine accomplishment comes from submitting our will to God's. God says, I can do remarkable things through you if you will depend on Me.

So God may build the right sort of confidence and self-esteem in us through the successes and rewards we receive when we are dependent upon Him. But even here the risks are great. An indulged Israel began to take God's love for granted. Even Gideon was not well served by his newfound confidence. When he became something other than the timid man he once had been, he created many problems for himself. God always takes a tremendous risk in blessing us!

Louis Evans Sr. recognized the tightrope that God walks between blessing us and keeping us dependent upon Him. In a prayer he wrote for weddings, he said, "Require of them, O Lord, such things as will bring them your blessing and develop their characters as they walk together." We might note that blessing and the building of character don't necessarily always happen together. So he added, "Give them enough tears to keep them tender, enough hurts to keep them human, enough failure to keep their hand clenched tightly in thine, and enough of success to make them sure they walk with God." Bad things in our lives may keep us tender, human, and dependent upon God. But our success gives us the confidence that we walk with God.

A third benefit we might receive from God's blessing is a taste of His glory. This is a wonderful thing. What is it that God wants to give us? In the good things in our lives we begin to taste and desire those gifts. When the apostle Paul said to fix our attention on "whatever is true, whatever is noble, whatever is right, whatever is pure, whatever is lovely, whatever is admirable—if anything is excellent or praiseworthy—think about such things" (Philippians 4:8), he was urging us to savor the things that are truly good in our lives, the things that incline us toward heaven where excellence and beauty reflect the heart of God Himself.

Each of us is drawn toward the things we think about. If we focus on shallow, short-term, earthbound pleasures, we are drawn down toward earth. But if we focus on what God reveals of the good and the beautiful, we are drawn by those good things toward heaven itself. So God can use good in our lives to draw us toward Himself, to make us anticipate the grand rewards that He promises us.

SURVIVING THE RISKS OF PROSPERITY

These are a few of the ways in which God uses an abundance of good things in our lives for a good end. But given the enormous risks, it is worth asking, How *does* one survive prosperity? How can we glean what is good and avoid the tremendous risks we are talking about that come through abundance? Jesus suggested to His disciples that "it is easier for a camel to go through the eye of a needle than for a rich man to enter the kingdom of God" (Matthew 19:24). The disciples were astonished at that. *How could anybody who has the world's wealth ever get into heaven?* they wondered. Can we find anyone in the Scriptures who has truly learned to abound?

I would like to suggest that Abraham was such a man. Back in Genesis 22 God placed an incredible challenge before Abraham, from which we can learn something profound. Abraham was fabulously wealthy. He had all the world's goods. He had God's blessing wherever he went. Whole nations and tribes were in awe of this nomad because of his great wealth and the obvious presence of God with him. How did Abraham learn to thrive in the midst of abundance? How did he learn to walk blamelessly before God in spite of the temptations of his wealth? We can learn the key through considering his life —and I believe that what we find in Genesis 22 is the *only* way you and I can survive abundance.

> Some time later God tested Abraham. He said to him, "Abraham!"
>
> "Here I am," he replied.
>
> Then God said, "Take your son, your only son, Isaac, whom you love, and go to the region of Moriah. Sacrifice him there as a burnt offering on one of the mountains I will tell you about." (vv. 1–2)

I can't even imagine how stunned Abraham must have been. First of all, he knew that his God was not a God of human sacrifice. Yet the word apparently came to him clearly and powerfully. God was going to test Abraham to see whether he could survive abundance. So God singled out Abraham's greatest blessing, the one he had spent his life anticipating, the one that gave a purpose to his accumulation of wealth, namely his dearly loved son and heir. We must see this in the context of a Middle Eastern culture where everything depended upon having an heir. So God was saying, "I want you to take the thing that is most precious to you and I want you to give it back to Me."

When Abraham heard the word, we are not told what is in his heart, but we can imagine it as he responds.

> Early the next morning Abraham got up and saddled his donkey. He took with him two of his servants and his son Isaac. When he had cut enough wood for the burnt

offering, he set out for the place God had told him about. On the third day Abraham looked up and saw the place in the distance. He said to his servants, "Stay here with the donkey while I and the boy go over there. We will worship and then we will come back to you."

Abraham took the wood for the burnt offering and placed it on his son Isaac, and he himself carried the fire and the knife. As the two of them went on together, Isaac spoke up and said to his father Abraham, "Father?"

"Yes, my son?" Abraham replied.

"The fire and wood are here," Isaac said, "but where is the lamb for the burnt offering?"

Abraham answered, "God himself will provide the lamb for the burnt offering, my son." And the two of them went on together. (vv. 3–8)

Abraham did not hesitate, even when his young son's bewildered questions must have torn open his heart.

When they reached the place God had told him about, Abraham built an altar there and arranged the wood on it. He bound his son Isaac and laid him on the altar, on top of the wood. Then he reached out his hand and took the knife to slay his son. But the angel of the Lord called out to him from heaven, "Abraham! Abraham!"

"Here I am," he replied.

"Do not lay a hand on the boy," he said. "Do not do anything to him. Now I know that you fear God, because you have not withheld from me your son, your only son." (vv. 9–12)

Up till the last possible moment, God tested Abraham to know what is in his heart, and what He found was that Abraham really was ready to let the most precious thing in the world go if God demanded it. And this, I believe, was the key to why, unlike many of us, God could bless Abraham with such abundance without destroying him. God could bless Abraham abundantly because, and *only* because, Abraham was *willing to let it go.* I do not believe you and I can survive prosperity unless we are willing to let it go.

The fact is, you and I cannot fully enjoy anything we do not hold with an open hand. It creates anxiety in us; it causes us to plot for the protection of those things we believe we own. This is true whether we are talking about our wealth or property, our career, our reputation, our health, our pleasures, our special opportunities, or even our children. If we hold onto these things, if we insist that we must have the right to protect them and keep them for ourselves and for our own advantage, if we become dependent upon them for our happiness, they will destroy us, and God knows that. This is because the moment we refuse to let go of *anything,* we have made it an end in itself. And the end for which we were created was nothing less than the ultimate fulfillment of a relationship with God. "Good things" in our lives are good only to the extent that they lead to and nurture the ultimate good, and that is our relationship with God. The moment they become a substitute for that, we have fallen into idolatry, and it will destroy us.

This is why Jesus, out of His genuine love for the rich young man who came to Him, said, "One thing you lack. Go, sell everything you have and give to the poor, and you will have treasure in heaven. Then come, follow me" (Mark 10:21). But the young man couldn't do it and went away deeply grieved. The *only* reason he couldn't do it was that the wealth meant more to him than a relationship with God did. That was the choice he had to make on the spot. Had that not been true, he could have let go of his wealth, as Abraham was willing to let go of his most treasured possession. It doesn't mean he would have lived his life in poverty. Abraham didn't. It might have meant that, of course, but then again it might not. The point is it would not have mattered because in that act he would have been expressing his trust that God would care for him every day of his life and give him everything that would actually serve his best interest.

The writer to the Hebrews in the New Testament tells us Abraham reasoned that if God wanted him to have a son and heir, as He had promised, then He was able to raise him from the dead, if necessary (Hebrews 11:19). Abraham's ultimate confidence was that God would provide. "Jehovah Jireh," he called the place— "The Lord Will Provide" (Genesis 22:14). And of course God did provide, not through resurrection as he anticipated, but through a ram, a substitute that took the place of his son. And here is God's conclusion: "I swear by myself, declares the Lord, that because you have done this and have not withheld your son, your only son, I will surely bless you" (vv. 16–17). You see, God desperately desires to express His love to us by blessing us. He wants to build our confidence by giving us success. He wants us to anticipate His glory in the good things we enjoy from day to day. But He also knows those things may destroy us. The *only* people He can bless so generously without destroying them are those who will hold His blessings with an open hand—those who show their confidence in Jehovah Jireh, God the Provider, by being generous in return. This I believe with all my heart: *The only way for you and me to survive abundance and escape the peril of prosperity and its destructive effect on our souls is to be a generous people,* to hold whatever God gives us, wealth or blessing or other good things, with an open hand, to share them generously, to be as generous in response as God has been in His generosity to us. If we will not, we would be far better off to be spared God's blessings in the first place.

"Give and it will be given to you," Jesus said. "A good measure, pressed down, shaken together and running over, will be poured into your lap. For with the measure you use, it will be measured to you" (Luke 6:38). "God loves a cheerful giver," the apostle Paul added. "And God is able to make all grace abound to you, so that in all things at all times, having all that you need, you will abound in every good work. . . . You will be made rich in every way so that you can be generous on every occasion" (2 Corinthians 9:7b, 8, 11).

Paul ended his letter to the Philippians by saying, "I love your generosity and I benefit from it. But in fact you are the greatest beneficiaries because of what God does in your hearts when you become a generous people." God can indeed use good things in our lives to accomplish His great and good purposes, but it could be the toughest thing we'll ever face.

NOTE

1. C. S. Lewis, *The Screwtape Letters* (New York: Macmillan, 1982), 132–33.

THRIVING IN A BROKEN WORLD

*A*ll this is a fascinating study, but in the end we must ask ourselves, What difference does it make in my life to know that God has promised to work in all things for the great good of those who love Him? Well, in the first place, I want to be numbered among those who truly love God. This is a simply enormous goal, and we hardly know where to begin, but from Moses in the Old Testament to Jesus in the New, God has made it clear that there is no more significant calling. Whatever else we do, we were created for the incomparable purpose of learning to love God with all our heart, soul, mind, and strength. With that pursuit comes God's promise of ultimate protection and ultimate joy. "God's plan for our good" begins and ends with the invitation to enter into an intimate, exhilarating, personal communion with the living God!

To love Him, of course, means much more than feeling sentimental about Him. It means that we will trust Him to have His way with us. His goal is to use whatever means are necessary and effective to shape us in His image, so that we might truly come to reflect His glory and enjoy Him forever. Vitally involved with loving Him, then, is my willingness to surrender to Him in obedience, and to be malleable in His hands. He knows what I need, of course, but it seems likely that the less malleable I am, the greater the possibility that I will need to be broken in order to be remade with the capacity to enjoy His glory.

But in the end, this promise, if I believe it, makes me the world's greatest optimist! I have always believed that the true Christian is a short-range pessimist because he knows he lives in a broken world, but a long-range optimist because he knows that God is redeeming that world. The true believer is realistic about the fact that the world is not getting better under its own power, but at the same time is free from the anxiety and fear that grip those who have no assurance that they are in the hands of a sovereign and loving God.

The great news of Romans 8:28 is that those who have surrendered to God's embrace can not only survive, but thrive in this broken world. For we have been assured a great deal more than some distant Paradise in an elusive afterlife. We have been promised the company of a sovereign God who is immediately and personally involved in every circumstance of our current lives to accomplish a great good beyond our imagining. Accompanied by such a God, I need not pine away for some eschatological deliverance at the end of days. My life today, for better and for worse, is part of the grand adventure that He has guaranteed will end one day in a place of indescribable glory. Nobody ever said our climb to the pinnacle would be without effort, danger, and possibly even great loss. But we have been promised that the view from the top will be worth it all.

REVIEW AND STUDY GUIDE

INTRODUCTION

*T*he purpose of the Foundations of the Faith series is to reacquaint the reader with some of the great doctrines and favorite Scripture passages relating to our Christian life. Indeed, these books attempt to link together our faith as we understand it and our life as we live it. Though our goal is to provide more in-depth teaching on a topic, we hope to accomplish this with a popular style and practical application. Books in the series include the *Lord's Prayer,* the *Beatitudes,* and *Psalm 23.*

In keeping with our goal of a popular-level treatment, this review and study guide is not meant to involve exhaustive digging, but to reinforce the important concepts (through "Points to Consider") and to help you explore some of their implications (through "Questions and Response").

A book's impact is judged in the long term, and if you can retain at least one important point per chapter and answer and act upon some of the questions relevant to your life, you have made considerable progress. May God bless your walk with Him as you enter into these exercises.

JAMES S. BELL JR.

Chapter One

POINTS TO CONSIDER

1. We naturally ask why a good and all-powerful God could allow senseless tragedy, and the answers are not always forthcoming.

2. Our questions fail in two key respects: God does not need to intervene in ways we think necessary to establish His justice, nor do we always understand the nature of the good or evil in various circumstances.

3. If God intervened to overrule our bad choices, our choices would not have value or meaning and we would never learn from the consequences.

4. Only God Himself sees the larger picture related to good and evil, and He can, in the long run, bring a greater good out of bad circumstances than we could ever imagine or construct ourselves.

5. If we live in a world that has fallen in every way, we should see the logic of some pain involved in making things right, in bringing about healing.

QUESTIONS AND RESPONSE

1. Why would you not be able to grow as a person if God intervened in all your negative circumstances? How, through God's allowing trials in your life, have you been able to reach a greater potential?

2. When have you been fooled into thinking you could judge the difference between good and evil in a given situation? Why did the outcome surprise you?

Chapter Two

Points to Consider

1. Though disasters and tragedies sometimes shake the conviction that there is a God in control, the concept of a mindless universe does not explain such things as order and reason.

2. Not only is God in control of every circumstance and detail in the universe, but His actions are not compromised by anything we do to oppose Him.

3. When God acts sovereignly through every detail, it is always for the good of His children; without His control in the little things, nothing important can be accomplished.

4. God's divine power and goodness are so broad that He can allow ugly distortions made by His creatures to fit into His plan to accomplish His great purposes.

5. Because God allows the tragedy due to sin, life is full of risk and even terror, but is also an adventure that ends with great reward for those who love God.

Questions and Response

1. What important events in your own life would have turned out differently if God had "missed" a small detail? When did God's direct intervention or leading make all the difference?

2. What limitations on your freedom have actually been a blessing in disguise? How did God get your attention in these circumstances?

Chapter Three

1. No matter what good God has planned, it seems that He allows us to "mess it up" in a way that at least appears to subvert His purposes.

2. The Bible doesn't ask whether we are free or determined but rather whether we are slaves to sin or slaves to God.

3. Free will implies almost an independence from God and the ability to make choices apart from Him, when only God Himself is capable of self-determination.

4. True freedom is not found in doing whatever we desire but in what God wills, allowing ourselves to be and do precisely what God created us for.

5. Jesus Christ was not bound to anything but was perfectly free; yet this freedom was a reality precisely because He submitted completely to the Father.

Questions and Response

1. What does true freedom mean to you? Do you experience it by doing what you enjoy most or by serving God? What is the difference in the long run as opposed to the short-term?

2. How do God's sovereignty and our freedom work in harmony? Why is this a win-win situation where great things can be accomplished?

Chapter Four

1. There are many unchangeable "givens" in life that we waste time trying to change, because we think the "what ifs" would make our lives better.

2. God's purposes in our circumstances are used to make us into creatures of exquisite glory, being able to more perfectly reflect and take delight in His own glory.

3. One purpose of the Scriptures is for us to clearly see how God keeps His covenant promises to His people, individuals who profit from God's care in both the good times and the bad.

4. God works in visible ways, such as the pillar of fire by night, but also invisible ways, such as angels guarding Israel against her enemies.

5. If you truly believe that God is working everything in your life for your good, then you will experience a tremendous release from fear and anxiety and the need to shoulder the burden yourself.

QUESTIONS AND RESPONSE

1. The author states that your sharing a meal with someone has the potential of greater significance than even a national event. What small things can you do to bless others that might have greater implications?

2. When a challenge, trial, or problem occurs, do you really believe God is in control and using it completely, or do you get worried and fearful? Why?

Chapter Five

POINTS TO CONSIDER

1. The characters in the story of Esther used their best efforts to achieve their own ends, and yet certain factors set in motion by God achieved His purposes in the end.

2. It's clear in the Esther story that God works it all together, but it is also apparent that the characters are not mere puppets being manipulated.

3. Our lives are like a tapestry in which God weaves all the individual threads, but at times a single thread, in isolation, may appear not to fit into a beautiful picture.

4. At times, our view of the tapestry (as opposed to God's heavenly view) is like seeing it from the back side, where the threads appear to make a random, chaotic pattern that doesn't make sense.

5. Our word "synergy" relates to the word used in Romans 8:28 and gives a clearer picture of individuals working to achieve more together than they could separately.

QUESTIONS AND RESPONSE

1. What have been some of the wonderful finished pictures or tapestries in your life that began in a difficult or chaotic way? What does this show you about God's sovereignty and purposes?

2. Where in your own life have you seen the principles of synergy? How have seemingly unrelated things had positive effects on each other? How does this illustrate the principle of Romans 8:28?

Chapter Six

1. Though God promises to work everything to the good in our lives, He does not promise that nothing bad will occur in life's circumstances or that we will never experience pain or failure.

2. Good has no definition apart from God, because who God is and what He does is the only way to define what is good.

3. When God is providing for our good, He is expressing His delight in us, bringing about prosperity and favorable circumstances in our lives so that we may enjoy the best of what He intends.

4. The process of everything moving in the direction of good is like a continual beginning, a movement from darkness to light, death to life, and despair to hope.

Questions and Response

1. C. S. Lewis stated that evil is a parasite—that it can only exist as a distortion of the good. Explain how many of the evils of our culture are subtle, appearing as agents of good, but actually feeding off it and spoiling it.

2. If some gourmet meals contain "nasty" ingredients, how have some of your best experiences contained setbacks, trials, disappointments, etc.?

Chapter Seven

POINTS TO CONSIDER

1. The hardest thing to do in life is to love God with everything in us; instead, we want to love ourselves or some other cause, all to our own loss.

2. Those who are advanced in loving God rejoice even when they experience temporal losses, because His love for us never wavers and our love for Him is not dependent upon His rewards but only upon Himself.

3. We tend to relentlessly pursue happiness, but it is never fully obtainable. The real goal should be joy, which is the state of satisfaction in God Himself.

4. God proved His great love for us because He laid down His life for us; likewise, if we do not love those around us in the same way, we cannot truly love God.

QUESTIONS AND RESPONSE

1. Give an example of someone you know who exhibited deep love for God under trying circumstances. What kind of understanding of God's love does that person have that you wish you had to a greater degree?

2. Go back to the quote by Thomas Watson about why we should love God. Which of his reasons most inspires you, and why? How does this change your diminished view of God?

Chapter Eight

POINTS TO CONSIDER

1. As human beings we are a quantum leap in importance above the rest of creation, being made in God's image and enjoying a special position in the eternal order of things.

2. It is evident that we share in God's creativity based upon the accomplishments of the human race and that we are given the privilege of managing what we have made as well as the forces of nature.

3. God has made things work in a certain way in everything from sexuality to spirituality, and if we try an illicit approach our temporary gratification will only lead to failure and destruction.

4. When we turn away from God's calling we become slaves to sin; we cannot come back to His purposes without the aid of His grace and power of His spirit.

QUESTIONS AND RESPONSE

1. When have you accepted Satan's lie that God's rules would keep us from happiness and fulfillment? What were the consequences of this false belief?

2. Have you ever sensed that some of your accomplishments had the hand of God stamped on them? How does God participate because we are in His image?

Chapter Nine

POINTS TO CONSIDER

1. Those of us who have been indulged in life will grow bored of what costs no effort, but those who suffer or pay a price will greatly appreciate what is sought.

2. We look forward to an eternal Paradise that is free from the limitations and corruptions of this present creation, which in itself would have been glorious if we had not sinned in the first place.

3. The glorious news is that our new bodies will be like His glorious body and that we will have incredible power to explore and manage His new universe, experiencing the complete ecstasy within it that God intends.

4. No matter how wonderful we picture heaven to be, it will be even better, because we cannot imagine a world that is better than God is capable of making.

QUESTIONS AND RESPONSE

1. How often do you meditate upon heaven and the purpose that God has for you for eternity? How might the joy of this hope lead you to be more diligent and obedient to His will here and now?

2. Of the things you have hoped for and received, have you appreciated those things that came at personal cost? Why or why not?

Chapter Ten

POINTS TO CONSIDER

1. Though we desire to have our hearts fixed on God's glory, the reality is that we are more fixed upon our own advancement, and the only solution is brokenness before God.

2. All of us want to think there is some good in us, but the purpose of the Law is to demonstrate that only God is good and that we cannot rely on ourselves to please Him, but only on Christ.

3. When sin's power begins to control us, we do not want to think that we are unable to escape its grasp and that it can ultimately destroy us, but without repentance and the power of Christ this is the case.

4. Numerous blessings result if we are willing to learn from our failures. The greatest benefit is the willingness to allow God to do whatever it takes to build Christlikeness in our lives.

QUESTIONS AND RESPONSE

1. Has God worked more powerfully in your life through brokenness or through your own gifts and strengths? Why is brokenness necessary, at least at certain times?

2. As you look at the long list of lessons from failure, which three have you best learned and applied to your life? Which three do you still most need to learn? What is holding you back?

Chapter Eleven

POINTS TO CONSIDER

1. No matter what type of tragedy may enter our lives, though we may not be able to alter the circumstances, we have the ability to choose how we will respond—allowing us to either grow or stagnate spiritually.

2. One of the purposes of suffering is to more clearly appreciate the beauty of the other areas in our lives that remain intact but that we regularly take for granted, and this includes God Himself.

3. Suffering also allows us to do the meaningful things in life with a greater sense of purpose as opposed to mere duty, recognizing the inherent worth of relationships and tasks and valuing them at a deeper level.

4. God lets our negative reactions to suffering, our anger, self-pity, and despair, draw us closer to Him as we further realize our own inadequacies and the depth of our sinfulness.

QUESTIONS AND RESPONSE

1. How have your own negative reactions to suffering further made you realize your need to depend on God rather than continuing to be angry or act as God's judge? How has this humbling strengthened you?

2. What relationships among family, friends, co-workers, etc., have become closer through the shared experience of suffering? How do you relate differently to each of these people?

Chapter Twelve

1. We think that if God revealed His presence more often we would have greater faith and obedience, but events in Scripture prove the opposite is true.

2. The reality is that God speaks clearly and continually, but we often do not want to listen, perhaps because we don't want to change in ways that God wants us to.

3. In God's seeming silence He is like a divine parent who wants us to act from what we have previously learned—to grow into maturity by learning to walk by faith rather than constant prompting from Him.

4. Though we often feel we are on our own when going through difficult times, we have a great group of witnesses watching as God gives us the grace to be overcomers against our flesh and the devil.

QUESTIONS AND RESPONSE

1. When have you had to obey God or make a difficult decision when His presence or direction was not perceived? What was the outcome, and what did you learn?

2. Is your main motivation in obeying God because you love Him and He commands you, or because of the blessings and rewards you receive? What does this say regarding your relationship to Him?

Chapter Thirteen

POINTS TO CONSIDER

1. Prosperity can be a more severe test of our faithfulness to God than suffering, because we no longer feel a dependence or need for Him.

2. Some of the negative aspects of prosperity include complacency, pride, corruption, self-indulgence, lack of compassion, and a sense that all these good things are a result of our own efforts or goodness.

3. If we are not willing to let go of what we possess, we have made it an idol upon which we depend for happiness. Rather than liberating us, it will destroy us.

4. The greatest escape from the many perils of prosperity is to be generous with what God has given to us, in the same spirit or proportion that He gave it to us in the first place.

QUESTIONS AND RESPONSE

1. Regardless of whether you are continually prosperous, when has prosperity (however limited) caused some of the wrong attitudes listed above? If it has not, how did you avoid these attitudes?

2. How do you view your own possessions in terms of giving? Do you view God as owning all of them and being generous with you, intending you to do the same?

Be sure to read all of the titles in the "Foundations of the Faith" Series:

All You Need to Believe
The Apostles' Creed
C. Donald Cole
0-8024-3053-8

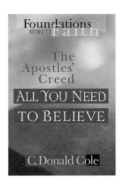

With the vast array of religions and beliefs
erupting in the world, how can we be sure of
what we believe? How can we defend our
beliefs using the Bible, not just from tradition?
Read about how the Apostles' Creed presents
the truths of the Gospel.

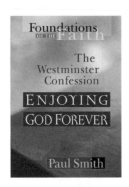

Enjoying God Forever
The Westminster Confession
Paul Smith
0-8024-7109-9

Discover afresh the truth of the Bible and the
passionate commitment to it held by the men
who authored the Westminster Confession.

On Our Knees and In His Arms
The Lord's Prayer
Peter Lewis
0-8024-3051-1

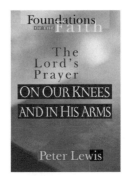

The Lord's Prayer is an important part of our
Christian heritage. More than mere tradition,
the prayer is a glimpse into the very Person
and purposes of God. Learn why we pray and
how the world is changed through prayer.

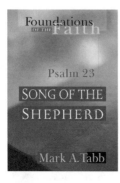

Song of the Shepherd
Psalm 23
Mark A. Tabb
0-8024-6190-5

If God is to be our Shepherd, we need to be His sheep. We must surrender our stubborn wills to His direction, bow to His discipline, and acknowledge His sovereignty over all heaven and earth. Learn how to live each day rendered to our Shepherd.

Love Full Circle
The Golden Rule
Doug McIntosh
0-8024-3054-6

"Do unto others as you would have them do unto you." Jesus used the Golden Rule to help people cut through the distractions and focus on what's most important to God. McIntosh explains how this concept simplifies the awesome message of Christ.